GIRL POWER!

Dedicated to all our fans, family and friends

THANKS
Rebecca Cripps
Rebecca Carroll
Carl Drummond
Simon Fuller
James Freedman
Danielle Fynn
Howard Johnson
Lou Pepper
Katherine Tulloh

PHOTOGRAPHY
Liz Johnson-Arthur
Simon Fuller
Jeff Bender
Ray Burmiston
Francessca Sorrenti
Ellen Von Unwerth
Kunihiro Takuma

DESIGN
 Tim Barnes

First published in 1997 by
ZONE/CHAMELEON BOOKS
an imprint of Andre Deutsch Ltd
106 Great Russell Street
London WC1B 3LJ

in association with
19 MANAGEMENT

SPICE GIRLS MANAGEMENT
Simon Fuller at 19 MANAGMENT

CIP data for this title is available from the British Library

ISBN 0233 991 654

Printed and bound in France

A Zone Production

GIRL
POWER!

Welcome...

...to **GIRL POWER!**

This is the only book that's written by all of us especially for all of you. This is the only place where you'll find out exactly what us Spice Girls are really like; what we think, what we love, what we hate, how we live. Everything you read on these pages is the way we see it and you know that anything we do for you is always totally honest, totally happening and 100% pure Spice!

Thanks for making sure that the Spice Squad is here to stay, and enjoy our first ever Spice book. And remember. The future is female!

Lots of love...

Melanie xCx

Victoria xix

Mel

Geri

Emma

GIRL POWER IS WHEN...

You help a guy with his bag

You and your mates reply
to wolf whistles by shouting
"Get your arse out!"

You wear high heels
and think on your feet

You know you can do it
and nothing's going to stop you

You don't wait around
for him to call

You stick with your mates
and they stick with you

You're loud and proud even when
you've broken out in spots

You believe in yourself
and control your own life

GIRL POWER!

I'VE GOT GIRL POWER BECAUSE...

 "...I was engaged, but broke away and found myself and my friends when I realised he wasn't right for me."

 "...I play football even though a lot of people turn their noses up at girls' football."

 "...I expect an equal relationship where he does just as much washing-up as I do (if not more)!"

 "...I appreciate that I am mixed race and I follow my own roots."

 "...I try and make the best of what I've got – even if I'm small, I think tall."

GIRL POWER!

FIRST IMPRESSIONS

21st July 96 SUNDAY 8.30 NIGHT

Just found out were no1

MEL B
"I thought **Emma** was a softie, butter-wouldn't-melt-in-my-mouth type, **Vicky** was a snob, and **Geri** was a real loudmouth. I knew **Mel C** was cool because she was my mate from Up North."

1st wardrobe performance of

T.O.T.P.

VICTORIA
"I thought **Mel C** was genuinely nice and **Geri** was mad (I'd never met anyone who dressed like that before). I'd known **Emma** for a long while and really liked her and I though **Mel B** was really pretty."

28796 BEFORE CAPITAL SUMMER JAM

SPICE GIRLS STILL No 1!

in our VAN

recand G after a hard trip feeling very very irritable

25th July

EMMA

"I thought **Victoria** was a bit of a snob (but all right) and that **Mel C** was really nice – she'd entertain me and dance round the room. I thought **Geri** was a nutter – she was wearing red short dungarees with stripey socks and massive shoes. I thought **Mel B** was incredibly cool."

MEL C

"I thought **Victoria** was gorgeous but a bit dim and **Geri** was a complete nutter. She had her hair in bunches and was wearing a pink fluffy jumper and saying 'Look, look – I'm a duck!' I thought **Emma** was just very sweet and **Mel B** was really cool because she was from Leeds."

GERI

"I thought **Victoria** was a bit odd when I met her at the 'Tank Girl' audition – everyone else was in fishnet tights and she came in wearing a suit. I could immediately feel **Mel C**'s dancer's presence when I met her. I was overwhelmed by **Mel B**'s massive brown eyes and thought she was very beautiful. I couldn't stop staring at **Emma** – she was really fresh and pretty with a big smile like a doll's."

10

"I'm not a pop star"

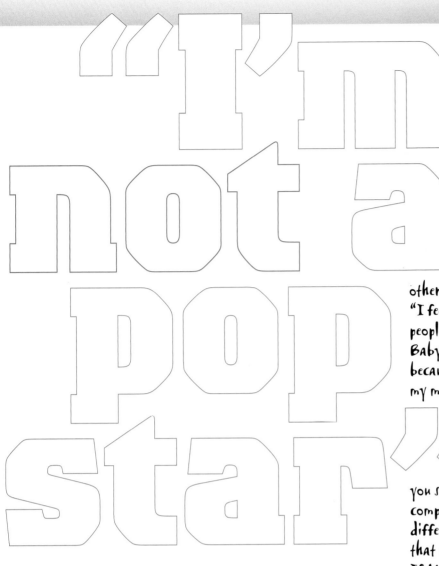

"Even though I was the last to join Spice Girls, I felt at home right away. I actually knew Vicky from when we were eight and did a show together, so she was a familiar face. We'd even been to our first gig together, to see Bobby Brown. My first night with the girls was my first time away from home and I got a bit homesick, so I went and had a cry on Geri's shoulder. That linked us and it's been the same with all the other girls.

"I feel very comfortable in the group now, but people still think I'm shy. I guess that's the Baby Spice thing, but that name only stuck because I love wearing my baby dolls, I love my mum and I love spending time in my bedroom. That's no act, because none of us pretend to be something we're not, but I'm not particularly shy. What you see is what you get. Our first management company tried to dress us the same and give us different songs to sing, but we couldn't do that even if we wanted to; we're too imperfect. If Mel C wants to wear trakkie bottoms, then why shouldn't she? And why should I wear something that's uncomfortable and I probably look hideous in?

"The appeal of Spice Girls is our honesty. We're not perfect and people like us for that. We make mistakes, fall over, scratch our arses – and I don't care who knows it! Well, except for George Clooney. He's gorgeous! Seriously though, we made a point of telling people we didn't want to be put on a pedestal right at the start.

"I suppose I'm fairly used to the spotlight. I've been doing modelling since I was a child and really loved it. My mum put the money

My favourite word?

candyfloss

Emma

away for me, and I ended up using it to pay for drama school. I did a bit of acting, but I was always more into singing and dancing. I've written lyrics since I was small and I used to do things like invent my own radio stations and pretend I was a DJ, so I think it was fate that I'd end up in a group.

"I'm really excited by the success we've had, but I don't get cocky about it. I never thought I was really any good, so I've always worked really hard at it and I think I have to keep working for everything I get. I take everything one day at a time. Who knows how long this will last? At the end of the day the public choose what they want and the day will come when they don't like us any more. I don't worry about the future. In fact, I don't worry about the past either. You learn from everything that's happened to you, especially the bad stuff. Well, you hope you learn from it. Until you find yourself doing exactly the same thing, that is!

"What does Girl Power mean to me? It's about

"We're doing it, girls, so can you. Even if you have to shout a bit louder, barge through all these people, then do it."

"I don't want to be a cutie, I want to be a hot sexy bitch."

taking control of your life and having respect for both other people and yourself. When I first met the girls I'd been going out with a boy for a long time, but I quickly realised that he wasn't right for me and got rid of him. That was Girl Power in action, right there. Some people are really selfish and

THE FIRST TIME I...

...bought a record

The album of 'The Sound of Music'. The first record I slow-danced to was Janet Jackson's, 'Let's Wait A While'. It was also the first time I was really mad about someone and I remember the smell of him up until this day.

...got in trouble

I live on the third floor and when I was very young I'd run and talk to my friends over the balcony at night when my mum wasn't looking. Then she'd come back in and tell me off and try and make me go to sleep. I just kept going out and in the end I got in really big trouble. But I'm quite a good girl, really.

...saw a film more than once

'Grease'. I watched it over and over again – and 'Dirty Dancing'. I'm a big fan of 'Pollyanna' with Hayley Mills, and 'Annie'. I've seen them all!

...lied and got caught out

I was looking after my mum's passport and she said, "You've still got it, haven't you?" and I kept saying yes, of course. In a way, I wasn't lying, because I thought I did. But I'd lost it and got in trouble.

...appeared on stage

When I was about three or four, I did a ballet show. I was the actual swan and I had a big tutu and all the others had to dance around me. It was very exciting.

...wore make-up

Not until I was about fifteen.

...stayed out all night

When I was about fifteen. My friend and I used to say we were staying at each other's houses. Once we went to the park and sat under the stars all night. It was wonderful.

...fancied a pop star

I loved that song 'Come On Eileen' and quite fancied the lead singer of Dexy's Midnight Runners. I also fancied Matt Goss for a little while.

...went to a football match

I used to go and see my dad and older brother play in the local league from the age of about two.

...saw a live concert

Bananarama. It was good at the time. I was with my friend and although we were quite far back, it was really exciting just being out on our own.

...went abroad

I went abroad quite a lot when I was younger because I used to do catalogue modelling on location – Corsica, Lanzarote, Portugal. From the age of six until I was about twelve I went away every year for two weeks for shoots. It was brilliant, because there used to be about ten kids and we only worked every other day. I was very lucky.

...had a near-death experience

I got run over when I was about four or five and I've got a scar on my left knee to prove it. I was knocked unconscious and the next thing I knew someone was dragging me out from under a car. If it hadn't stopped, it would have gone over my head. Even now, I don't like it when cars get close as I'm crossing the road.

...wore a mini skirt

I always had little kilts, which I wore with fluffy jumpers.

...killed an animal

I had a baby bird once and my mum told me to feed it while she was away. Unfortunately, I'd spent all my money going out the night before, so I fed it some of my nan's bird food instead – only her bird is a parrot. When I came in the next morning it was on its back, I

> "When I was young I always wanted to work behind the counter of a shop. That's where I'd be now if I wasn't in Spice Girls."

felt terrible. It must have choked to death – horrible!

...got drunk

When I was about sixteen, sitting in the park with all my friends. I thought it was pretty cool at the time, but I felt dreadful afterwards.

...won a prize

We used to go to Clacton and stay in a caravan, partly because there were lots of things for kids to do. I won the Highfields Princess competition. It was quite nice – I had to sit on a big chair wearing a little crown!

...went to hospital

When I got run over.

...went to school

I didn't want my mum to leave and the teacher asked me why. I said: "Because I do!" So they dragged her out and left me there.

...fell in love

It wasn't long ago – about three or four years ago.

...failed an exam

I was very upset when I got G for my maths. I didn't even know I had an exam and I walked in and it all just went completely wrong

....got an A

In dance.

13

that pisses me off because I think I'm the caring sort. I like to make sure that everybody's alright, which was what the others were doing for me in that situation. "I still live in a flat with my mum and my brother, but I'm hoping to buy her a house soon. She's never had a garden, so she'll love that. I'll probably move in with her for a little while, then I'll get somewhere for myself when I'm ready. I really like living at home but I think the time will come when I need more of my own space. I must be getting old!

"Some people will probably always see me as Baby Spice, but I think others are already starting to have different opinions of me. One person will think I'm cute and one will think I'm dog-rough. Of course I'd love everyone to think of me as a sexy bitch, but I'm not sure that will ever happen. What was weird was that one of the national newspapers asked a load of girls who they would like to be out of all the women in the world. I came out on top! Now that really is bizarre. Imagine if their wishes came true and there were thousands of Emmas roaming the streets. That would be just too scary!" E

"I believe in something after death but I don't know what it is. There must be something afterwards and I hope I get there. So I do believe in it. I do, I do, I do!"

"Of course I'm a feminist. But I could never burn my **wonderbra**. I'm nothing without it!"

"Worst thing I've ever had in my mouth? A **wasp**, which stung me on my tongue. My tongue **swelled up** and I was quite ill."

"The best thing about getting back home is meeting up with your mates and going to the pub."

Best chat-up line:
"Do you wanna come down **Dunkin Donuts**?"

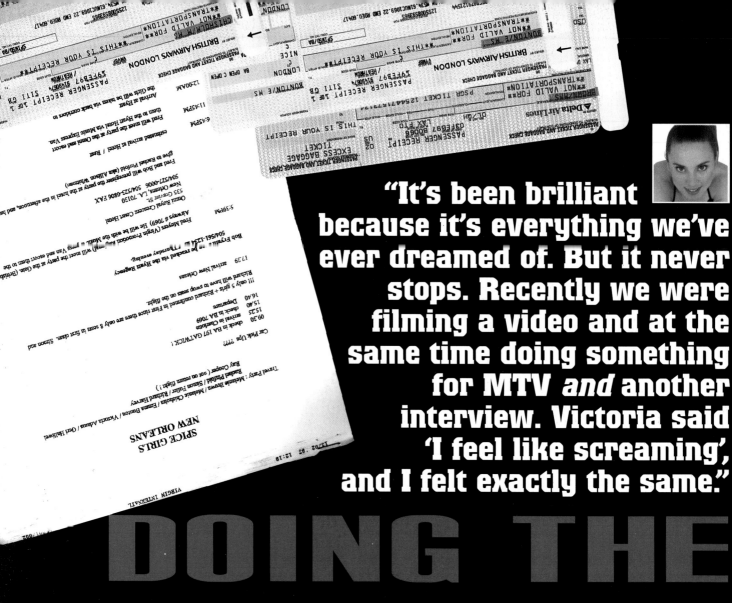

> "It's been brilliant because it's everything we've ever dreamed of. But it never stops. Recently we were filming a video and at the same time doing something for MTV *and* another interview. Victoria said 'I feel like screaming', and I felt exactly the same."

DOING THE

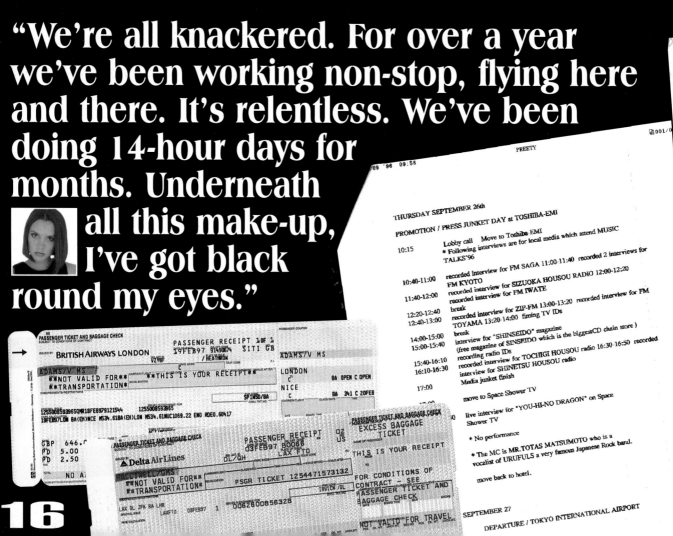

> "We're all knackered. For over a year we've been working non-stop, flying here and there. It's relentless. We've been doing 14-hour days for months. Underneath all this make-up, I've got black round my eyes."

PREETY

'09 '96 09:58

THURSDAY SEPTEMBER 26th

PROMOTION / PRESS JUNKET DAY at TOSHIBA-EMI

10:15 — Lobby call   Move to Toshiba-EMI
 * Following interviews are for local media which attend MUSIC TALKS'96

10:40-11:00 — recorded interview for FM SAGA 11:00-11:40 recorded 2 interviews for FM KYOTO

11:40-12:00 — recorded interview for SIZUOKA HOUSOU RADIO 12:00-12:20 recorded interview for FM IWATE

12:20-12:40 — break

12:40-13:00 — recorded interview for ZIP-FM 13:00-13:20 recorded interview for FM TOYAMA 13:20-14:00 filming TV IDs

14:00-15:00 — break

15:00-15:40 — interview for "SHINSEIDO" magazine (free magazine of SINSEIDO which is the biggestCD chain store)

15:40-16:10 — recording radio IDs

16:10-16:30 — recorded interview for TOCHIGI HOUSOU radio 16:30-16:50 recorded interview for SHINETSU HOUSOU radio
                Media junket finish

17:00 — move to Space Shower TV

       live interview for "YOU-HI-NO DRAGON" on Space Shower TV

       * No performance

       * The MC is MR.TOTAS MATSUMOTO who is a vocalist of URUFULS a very famous Japanese Rock band.

       move back to hotel.

SEPTEMBER 27
DEPARTURE / TOKYO INTERNATIONAL AIRPORT

> # "We get these schedules every day – on them is what we're doing every minute of the day, sometimes from 6.00am to midnight. You can't look at more than one at a time or you'd go mad."

BUSINESS

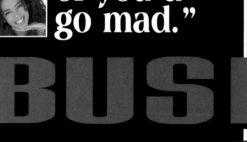

SPICE GIRLS
LAPLAND

...DULE FOR CONTESTWINNERS

...rsday December 4th

everybody to meet at Victoria station
Gatwick express entrance

...5   train departs for Gatwick

...5   arrive Gatwick

...0   check in at Gatwick South Terminal
zone A
European Aviation Check in desk
flight EAF 4358

...00   leave for Rovaniemi

...00   arrive Gotheborg - refuel + pick up more passengers

...00   leave for Rovaniemi

...8.20 Arrive Rovaniemi
Santa meets us upon arrival

*** luggage will go straight from airport to hotel ***

...8.50 coach leaves for Santa Village
...ls on separate coach

...19.00

** meet Santa +...

Photo...countries that have their own photographer to take pict...
santa

Franc...
Germ...
Japan...
Spain...
Port...
Finla...

20.0...

20.15   check in hotel

...97   04:04PM VIRGIN

9:00PM: Van should meet bus at the SKYLINE HOT...
            Return to hotel

TUESDAY, JANUARY 28

6:30AM: Passenger van arrives at hotel and will stay...
Music Express: 800.255.4444
7:15AM: On air interview at WKTU radio with morn...
            THAT Ru-Paul)
            525 Washington Boulevard
            16th Floor, Newport Towers
            Jersey City, NJ 07310
            201.420.3700 phone
Virgin contact: Andi Turco 917.846.4067 (mobile) 2...

9:00AM: Arrive at MJI Broadcasting studios
            MJI Broadcasting/Hit Fax
            Museum of Television and Radio
            25 West 52nd Street (between 5th & 6...
            New York, NY 10019
            212.621.6600
Virgin contact: Andi Turco 917.846.4067 (mobile...

Here is the confirmed information as of 1/24/97:

9:00AM: KDWB-MINNEAPOLIS, MINNESO...
9:30AM: WWZZ-WASHINGTON, DC
9:40AM: WPRO-PROVIDENCE, RHODE IS...
9:50AM: WXXL-ORLANDO, FLORIDA
10:00A...   KMYV-KANS... ITY, MISSOU...
            ..., RHO...
            ...ZONA
            ..., FL...
11:00AM: KHKS-...LAS, TEXAS
11:20AM: WRVQ-RICHMOND, VIRGINIA...
11:30A...   ...VEGAS
11:40A...   ...RANC...
11:50A...   ...IEGO

12:20PM: BREAK (lunch/free time)
...PM: ...INE IN...
            ...E 212....
Location: TBD
Virgin contact: Yon Elvira 212.332.0432

...Page 2 of 8

11:05 - 11:10 am -   Switch rooms

11:10 - 11:25 am -   *eNow/BBS (national weekly arts & entertainment show) - Pretaped
                       T.V.   Interviewer/contact: Liz West 299-2332

11:25 - 11:30 am -   Switch rooms

11:30 am - 11:45 am - CTV News Service/BBS/World Beat News (national evening news) -
                       Pretaped T.V.   Interviewer/contact: Mike Katryz 299-2226

11:45 - 11:50 am -   Victoria & Mel C to switch rooms for Images Magazine in-person i/v.
                       Geri, Mel B & Emma to their rooms for phoners.

11:50 am - 12:05 pm - *Images Magazine (national beauty/lifestyle monthly magazine) - Print.
                       Interviewer: Rhonda Rich 595-9944/537-3103 w/Victoria & Mel C

11:50 am - 12:05 pm - *HOT 103.5 (Top 40 Dance-oriented radio station) - LIVE PHONER
                       Interviewer: Adrian Bell Direct #:905-453-2915   w/Geri
                       (main:905-452-7111)

11:50 am - 12:05 pm - *Secondary Press (High School bi-monthly Youth magazine) - Print
                       phoner. Interviewer: Dan Moreale 905-546-1139   w/Mel B

11:50 am - 12:05 pm - *"Kids World" (Youth bi-monthly culture/entertainment magazine) -
                       Print phoner. Interviewer: Karen Bliss 944-0930   w/Emma

12:05 - 1:05 pm -   LUNCH BREAK

1:05 - 1:25 pm -   "Hit List"/YTV (national Top 40 youth TV) - Pretaped T.V.
                       Host: Tarzan Dan   contact: Terry Diachok 534-1191 ex.246

1:25 - 1:30 pm -   Switch hosts (same camera crew & set up)

1:30 - 1:45 pm -   YTV News (national Youth TV's weekly news show) - Pretaped T.V.
                       Interviewer/contact: Exan Augoung

1:45 - 1:50 pm -   Switch to other room.

1:50 - 2:00 pm -   Coffee Break - Meet with EMI Records' sales team at hotel (10 mins)

2:00 - 2:10 pm -   Group shot w/photograph for Tor... ... Switch...

2:10...   ... weekly ...n-person
                       ...viewer: Marc Weisbott 487-0660
                                                         w/Geri & Mel C

> # "Even though we moan a lot I believe we are the luckiest five girls on earth." **MEL B**

17

"I hate organisation in life. I want chaos and spur-of-the-moment action. I'm impulsive and strong-willed and I've got a foul mouth, which are all the qualifications you need to be in Spice Girls. I love what I do now, because there's something different happening every day. I had a job for two months doing telesales for a newspaper where I grew up in Leeds and it did my head in. There was no way I could live that nine-to-five lifestyle, so I was definitely cut out to be an entertainer.

"My mum's probably glad to have me off her hands, because I just had too much energy as a kid, I was a nutter. She had to pack me off to my aunt's every weekend because I was too much for her. That's why she sent me to dancing classes when I was eight too.

"I've had a weird and wild life before Spice Girls. I won a beauty competition, Miss Leeds Weekly News, when I was seventeen. My mum entered me without me knowing and when they asked me to be in the finals I wouldn't let my mum or dad come and watch. I only went and won it though, didn't I! I got a car for a year, even though I couldn't drive, and a trip to Disneyland. I took my boyfriend with me, and he eventually sold his story of our lovelife to the papers, the swine.

"I had a job in panto at the Lewisham Odeon in London for a while and got sacked because I kept giggling. It was a cheap production and there was only one mic to go round. One of the actors had the mic stuck in the middle of his forehead and so I had to say my lines to his head. I kept giggling. I couldn't help it. It was no good. My agent said I'd never work again because I'd been sacked, but I proved him wrong.

"I think it's fate that the five of us have been given the chance to be successful, because we're

"If you want to stand up and say 'Aaaargh' then do it. You decide the kind of life you want to lead."

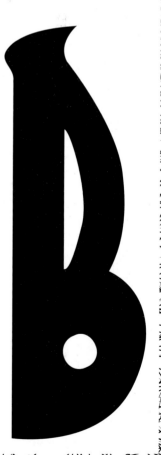

Favourite words?
higgledy-piggledy
&
hotch-potch
Maybe it's
a Leeds thing.

19

"I've always been a deep thinker. But then again, I'm loud and spontaneous and a bit of a twat sometimes, which doesn't really go with being a deep thinker."

✓ Best advice:

Please yourself and respect others.

My mum gave me a lot of advice, but mainly I've taken it on myself to come to my own conclusions. Sometimes I've got it drastically wrong, but I'm one of those people who has to find out for themselves.

✗ Worst advice:

Don't do it.

That's the worst advice anybody could ever give me. I hate the way some people try and conform, just because they're scared that they're going to make a bad impression. I say: just do it! It'll work out good in the end if you do it with a nice positive smile on your face.

"Every girl's got a right to stick up for herself."

GIRL POWER MEL. B

nothing like normal pop stars. The pop star life is all about stereotypes and fitting into a bracket and we don't want to do that. We don't want to work with the producer that everybody else is working with and we don't want to wear what everybody else is wearing. I really believe we should all do whatever the hell we like in this band. Not that I'm the driving force behind Spice Girls. Everyone brings a really strong quality to the group, whether it's in a very upfront way or something that's within them. It's just that I'm dead outspoken. Most people think before they speak. Not me. I just come out with whatever's going on in my brain. Sometimes I think 'God, that sounds really horrible' and I'll wish I hadn't said it, but that's the way I am. If I don't like you, I'll tell you.

"If I do like you, though, you're alright. My biggest achievement so far has been doing something for my family for once. My dad was made redundant recently, so I paid off their mortgage for them. It was just my way of saying 'sorry about being a brat when I was younger'. Money doesn't matter to me. I've always spent whatever I've earned. When I go into a shop I'll always buy something for whoever's with me... let them enjoy some of what I've got too. My house actually burned down not too long ago, but I didn't give a toss about my posses-sions. I was just freaked out because I could have been killed.

"I started going to a healer after that to try and make myself feel a bit

"Sex is the world."

Best chat-up line:
"Fancy a bevvy?"
Worst chat-up line:
"By 'eck, you smell gorgeous tonight, Petal."

21

THE FIRST TIME I...

...bought a record
'Mickey' by Toni Basil. The first record I snogged to was 'Endless Love' – quite a soppy one.

...got in trouble
When I was about eight – for nicking penny sweets from my corner shop. The shopkeeper told my mum!

...saw a film more than once
'The Wiz' with Michael Jackson and Diana Ross. It's excellent. If you haven't seen it, get it out on video. Its the best adventure musical – for kids, but not for kids.

...lied and got caught out
At school when I used to try and get past the dinner queue till without paying. I got caught, put on report and went to detention. I liked detention because all the naughty ones got left together and it was like a riot.

...appeared on stage
I must have been about six, in a drama competition. I wore a clown outfit and I played an American clown who really wanted to be a performer. I loved it, but my mum and her mate were in the background in hysterical laughter because they were so nervous. That really put me off.

...wore make-up
When I was six, because you wear make-up when you go on stage.

...stayed out all night
It was when I became Miss Leeds Weekly News and won a Renault Clio for a year, while I was at college doing contemporary dance. It was flesh night at the Hacienda, so I went with a load of friends, but I had to hide it from my mum because it was a gay night.

...fancied a pop star
I didn't really fancy anybody, apart from my dad's friend. I was about eight and I used to get really shy when he came round. He was lovely.

...went to a football match
My ex-boyfriend was a reserve in the Leeds United team, so I went to see Leeds and met David Batty and Vinnie Jones. You know they kick the ball about before it starts? Well about halfway through the game I asked my boyfriend whether it had started yet. It was so boring I couldn't tell the game from the warm-up!

...saw a live concert
I couldn't afford to go to concerts when I was younger, so the first was Janet Jackson with the other girls. It was excellent. She cried on stage and I thought she was getting really emotional, but then I found out she did it every night.

...saw an 18 film
'Porkies'. It was really crap!

...went abroad
I went away to Spain with my mum's dancing-class friend when I was thirteen. I got really ill and they left me in by myself while they went out. Prats!

...had a near-death experience
I thought I was nearly dying when I dislocated my knee during a school show. The good thing was that afterwards I had physiotherapy with loads of footballers every Saturday, so that made up for the pain! But then my dad had a knee operation and he started coming – it wasn't as good after that.

...wore a mini skirt
I had a ra-ra skirt. Horrible!

...killed an animal
My mum and sister thought that I actually killed my guinea pig, but I didn't. I used to kill spiders all the time, but nothing else.

...got drunk
I remember getting drunk on Babycham one Christmas – or I thought I was. I was very young at the time.

...won a prize
Miss Leeds Weekly News

...went to hospital
When I was six and I had a really bad eye infection. I had to go and see a specialist, because I couldn't actually open my eyes.

...went to school
On my first day at high school, my dad had told me which bus to get but I got off at the wrong stop. I was miles away from the school and so nervous that my mouth got really dry and my tongue felt frozen. I was late, for a start, and everyone was looking at me – a complete nervous wreck. I had to talk to myself and say: "It'll be alright! It'll be alright!" Poor thing – I had my hair in a bun and everything.

...fell in love
When I was thirteen years old, with the guy who's now sold a story about me. After that, I never really had love. I never used to get a lot of people falling in love with me, but I didn't want to be heavy because I'd already had a serious sweetheart. I just wanted a bit of fun and they always used to get serious on me, saying things like: "Let's wait a while before we kiss". I hated that – it did my head in. So I just used to go out with the girls then – or older men!

better; I'm really into spiritualism now. You get a lot of good karma from it, your whole soul feels cleansed. I've got a spirit guide now. She's kind of a guardian angel who keeps you in check, leads you to experiences that will take you to the next stage of life.

"It stops me worrying about anything now. I've got so many skeletons in my closet that if I sat fretting about them I couldn't get on with being a Spice Girl. I'm at peace with the way I am and I want to experience as much as possible. If I don't have a mad time and live the life then how the hell will I know if I like it or not?

"What shows I've got Girl Power? The fact that I'm really carefree on the outside. I once went out on a date

"The worst thing I've ever had in my mouth? When I was a kid, I used to pick up little stones and put them in my mouth. My mate at primary school had really long nails and they were really dirty. I wanted to be like her so I used to scratch my nails in the dirt and put little stones in my mouth. I also used to pick chewing gum up off the pavement and eat it! I wonder what that means?"

with someone who was painfully shy and by the end of the night we were sitting around chatting away completely naked! I can make people forget themselves and just chill out without even realising it. And that's very cool."

"The strong will survive and the wise excel."

OUR TUNES

"We really had to choose carefully which songs **MEL B** to put on the album as we've written about thirty-five. We really wanted the public to see the progression in our music and in our lyrics."

"I want people to think **MEL C** of us as the new Oasis."

"Creatively, I love lyrics. My main thing in the **G** group is that I come up with ideas. We've all got balls but I've got quite big balls, basically."

"Writing for other artists is very important. B **It's one thing we want to do and we really have got songs for other people."**

STAGE 2

"Whenever I hear one of our songs, I still E **get goose-pimples."**

"What's important is the message. There's a MEL B **colourful element that attracts the younger generation, but then if you want to read between the lines there is a funny, sick sense of humour there and a deeper message – if you want to get it."**

"When we write a song, we have a huge pad and we just write down ideas – even the most ridiculous silly things. We end up with a big page of phrases and words and put them all together. Every single song is MEL about things we've experienced since C growing up – situations we've been in with friends, with lads and with our parents. Because we've all had different experiences, you get lots of angles on everything."

25

MEL C

"We are what we are. We're not gonna change. We just take people by their vibe because that's all that matters."

"I'm very shy when I meet people and I have a recurring nightmare that someone will come up and start talking to me when I'm buying my tampax in the supermarket. It's a good job it hasn't happened yet, because I'd just die of embarrassment! You might not believe that from watching me on stage, because when I'm up there I'll do anything. It's not the same as a one-to-one encounter.

"The weirdest thing about everything that's happened to me in Spice Girls is that when I see a picture of myself in the papers it doesn't connect that it's me. It's the same when I watch a video. I think only I can see it and it doesn't register that all around the world millions of people are watching it too. It helps me keep my feet on the ground, I suppose. I never have any expectations and just take it all as it comes. Everything we do just seems to get bigger and bigger, but all I can think is that we're five dead normal girls just writing a few tunes. It's incredible that so many people have bought our CDs.

"A bloke's best chat-up line with me would be an invitation to a football match.

I'm not really interested in restaurants, romance and all that bollocks."

THE FIRST TIME I...

...bought a record
It was the 'Kids From Fame' album – it was brilliant. I used to do the whole show in my front room.

...got in trouble
I always used to get in trouble when I fought with my cousin. I'm really close to him now but we used to fight like cat and dog – or brother and sister. I bit and scratched him and he pulled my hair!

...saw a film more than once
'Flash Gordon' – I loved it. Me and my dad always go to the pictures and eat loads of popcorn together – that's like our little thing.

...lied and got caught out
Remember when everyone used to have those crap bright yellow rollerboots? Well, I only had rollerskates

and I used to lie and say, "Yeah, I've got rollerboots, but they're too good to wear out in the street." Then one of my friends came round and said in front of my mum, "Where are your rollerboots?". I didn't have any and I was really embarrassed. So I've never, ever lied again!

...appeared on stage
I first went to dancing when I was three, and that was when I did my first show. I sang 'Oh I Do Like To Be Beside The Seaside' with lots of knee bends and toe points.

...wore make-up
My mum's a singer and every Friday, Saturday and Sunday nights she goes out to a gig and puts all her make-up on. I used to love watching her do it. I was about nine or ten and no one in my class wore make-up – but when we had school discos I made my mum do me up like her. I'd go along with bright green eyeshadow on and pink lipstick, looking hideous! But apart from that, I've never been much of a make-up wearer, really.

...stayed out all night
When I left school and went away to college at sixteen, I left home as well. Before that, I didn't really go out a lot, because I was too young and couldn't get into clubs. I was too much into my dancing, anyway.

...fancied a pop star
Adam Ant was the first; George Michael came later.

...went to a football match
My dad took me to the match once when I was a baby, but I don't remember it.

...saw a live concert
Because I lived in Liverpool, I didn't go to many concerts – they were all in Manchester and you don't really travel that much when you're young, do you? So I didn't go to a concert until I came to London – it was Madonna's 'Girlie Show' tour and it was brilliant.

...saw an 18 film
'Rambo', I think. My older brothers always used to get lots of horror films on video and let me watch them too.

...went abroad
I've been quite lucky because my dad works for travel

"I seem to have come a long way from auditioning for endless chorus lines and not getting anywhere, although I never lost faith in myself. I'm not a great singer or a great dancer, but this is all I want to do, it's all I can do. I could never go and work in a shop, so I always found the strength to keep going. I'll always remember how fate took a hand though. I was down to the last five for a role in 'Cats' and couldn't go to the audition because I had tonsilitis. They rejected me and then almost straight away I joined Spice Girls, so how lucky was I? Even though I'd danced since I was three I'd always wanted to be pop star, so that was a lucky break. My mum was in a band called 'Love Potion' years ago and she even released a couple of singles, so I think it's in the blood. She still sings in the clubs today.

"The music is probably the only thing I take seriously about my life. I listen to our album every now and again and although I'm dead proud of it, I can't help cringing when I listen to a couple of bits where I think the singing's

✔ **Best advice:**
Believe in yourself.
My mum taught me that. All our mums are very supportive.

✘ **Worst advice:**
Get a perm.
When I was about fourteen I thought I was Neneh Cherry, so I went out and got a corkscrew spiral perm and it looked dreadful. And my hair's never been the same since.

companies and we've always gone away. When I was a toddler I went to Benidorm, I think.

...had a near-death experience
My cousin nearly drowned me in one of our fights – it was awful. He kept pushing me down and I was gasping, thinking, "I'm gonna die!". Apart from that and a couple of minor car crashes, I've been quite lucky, touch wood.

...wore a mini skirt
I went through a phase of wearing little skirts when I was about twelve – my legs were really skinny then.

...killed an animal
I used to kill flies by snapping them with elastic bands. One time I killed a really big bluebottle and felt guilty for weeks because it was really big - not just a fly, but a proper creature. I kept having dreams about this fly's family attacking me while I was asleep. I was also really worried about God being angry with me.

...got drunk
I was still at school – fifteen or sixteen – and we all went out. You know when you're a kid, and you save

up for about a month and you've got about £7? So I went out with £7 and the train fare was £1, so I was watching my purse from the start. But one of my friends was really rich and had £50, so we all got drunk on her! It was weird – you just get all giggly and stupid, don't you?

...won a prize
I always won gymnastics prizes because I always used to give it loads in the dance bits. I'm really shy and quiet, especially if you don't know me, but when it comes to performing, I find it a lot easier.

...went to hospital
I was quite accident-prone when I was little. I got the scar on my head when I was three and someone at nursery school pulled a chair out on my head and split it open. After I went to hospital and had stitches, the Social Services came round because they thought my mum and dad had been beating me up!

...went to school
I can remember my first day at high school. I was gutted because I was so nervous about it. A few days

before, I'd fallen off my brother's bike and got a terrible gash on my knee (I've still got the scar). I had to go and see the nurse, which meant that on my first day at school I had to be excused. It was really scary – and horrible to be limping around with this bloody knee.

...fell in love
My first love was at school. At the time, I really thought I was in love, but when I look back, I just think I was being a bit silly. But we're still really good friends and I love him to death.

...got an A
I don't think I ever got an A. I did well in my GCSEs – I got 4 Bs and 5 Cs - but I've never been academic. I've always just been into my dancing.

...failed an exam
I was always rubbish at tap, so I failed the tap exam, which is just never done, but I managed.

a bit ropey. I think there's a lot more to our music than most of the pop stuff we get lumped in with though. A lot of groups are just writing the stuff they think the public want, what's going to sell. We're not interested in that. We're just writing what we want to write. What kid wants to hear slushy stuff like 'I've never felt this way before'? What kind of person wants to hear that stuff?!

"I don't have musical heroes, but I'd really love to meet Madonna. I really, really admire her and I'd love to have a normal conversation with her, ask her how the baby is and all that. It's a bit weird really, because I'm not mad about her music and I didn't like the 'Sex' stuff either. I'm not prudish. I can talk about sex all day long, but when it's personal I get a bit shy. I'd be embarrassed getting my kit off. I'm actually bothered about my legs more than anything else, but I don't know why.

"Madonna's been doing her thing for so long, I'd like to think we could match that. It would be great to be together in ten years' time.

"This is a new attitude. Girls are taking control. If you want to wear a short skirt, then you go on and wear it."

We all want families so maybe we could take time out for that at some stage and then get back together. But who really knows? I like to have goals but it's pointless looking too far ahead. Maybe I'll wake up tomorrow and decide that I've had enough of Spice Girls.

"What could be better in my life? My love life. I know it will be difficult with the amount of work that we do, but I'm sure I'll find time. Not that I'm worried about it. One thing being in Spice Girls has taught me is that you don't necessarily need a man. Anyway, how can I complain? I think we're the five luckiest girls on the planet, so that's not too bad, is it? Mind you, it's really hard work. I was at home the other night watching telly and I was so tired that when I decided to go to bed, I couldn't physically stand up. I had to literally crawl to bed. No matter how tired I feel, though, I know I'll never stop performing. You can guarantee I'll be a sad old bag up on stage still trying to sing when I'm 60!"

THE ALBUM

WANNABE

WHAT'S THE STORY? "We were just having a laugh in the studio when we wrote Wannabe. It's **MEL B** more of a vibe song than anything else. It had no sit-down planning. The sentiment, the meaning, the lyrics, the rhythm, just happened."

"It was recorded in under an hour, **MEL C** whereas a lot of the other songs on the album took two or three days at least."

If you wanna be my lover you gotta get make it last forever, friendship

"We're about unity and solidarity between female friends."

G "We'd already written parts of it when Mel B and Emma came up with the bridge. It was a mad time – we got all excited because we knew we'd found something really good."

E "We've got a few private little words and phrases, like 'zigazig-ha', and we just twisted them up a bit for Wannabe."

Yo I'll tell you what I want, what I really really want
So tell me what you want, what you really really want
I'll tell you what I want, what I really really want
So tell me what you want, what you really really want
I wanna, I wanna, I wanna, I wanna, I wanna really
really really wanna zigazig-ha

If you want my future forget my past
If you wanna get with me better make it fast
Now don't go wasting my precious time
Get your act together we could be just fine

I'll tell you what I want, what I really really want
So tell me what you want, what you really really want
I wanna, I wanna, I wanna, I wanna, I wanna really
really really wanna zigazig-ha

If you wanna be my lover you gotta get with my friends
Make it last forever, friendship never ends
If you wanna be my lover you have got to give
Taking is too easy but that's the way it is

What do you think about that now you know how I feel
Say you can handle my love are you for real
I won't be hasty, I'll give you a try
If you really bug me then I'll say goodbye

I'll tell you what I want, what I really really want
So tell me what you want, what you really really want
I wanna, I wanna, I wanna, I wanna, I wanna really
really really wanna zigazig-ha

with my friends
never ends

If you wanna be my lover you have got to give
Taking is too easy but that's the way it is

So here's a story from A to Z, you wanna get with me
you gotta listen carefully
We got Em in the place who likes it in your face
We got G like MC who likes it in an
Easy V doesn't come for free she's a real lady
and as for me you'll see
Slam your body down and wind it all around
Slam your body down and wind it all around

If you wanna be my lover you gotta get with my friends
Make it last forever, friendship never ends
If you wanna be my lover you have got to give
Taking is too easy but that's the way it is

If you wanna be my lover, you gotta, you gotta, you gotta
you gotta, you gotta slam slam slam slam
Slam your body down and wind it all around
Slam your body down and wind it all around
Slam your body down and wind it all around
Slam your body down zigazig-ha
If you wanna be my lover

> "We never mean to offend anybody, we're just a bit naughty."
> MEL C

ZÍga ZÍG ⊕ aaah!

NO TTIN

ON VIDEO

"I remember the chaos and the cold. It wasn't very controlled – we didn't want it to be. We wanted the camera to capture the madness of Spice. I had very big shoes on and fell over many times. I watched it again recently and thought it was like a comedy, really. All the other girls gave me the award for being the biggest prat in it! It's the most spontaneous of our videos." GERI

Director: Jhoan Camitz   Location: St. Pancras, London

SPECIAL BECAUSE...
"...it was the first one to explode into the Spice-o-sphere." E

35

Say you'll be there
I'm giving you everything
All that joy can bring
this I swear

Last time that we had this conversation
I decided we should be friends
Yeah, but now we're going round in circles
Tell me will this deja vu never end
Now you tell me that you've fallen in love
Well I never ever thought that would be
This time you gotta take it easy throwing
far too much emotions at me
But any fool can see they're falling
I gotta make you understand

Say you'll be there
I'm giving you everything
All that joy can bring
this I swear

And all that I want from you is a promise you will be there

Say you will be there
Won't you sing it with me

If you put two and two together you
Will see what our friendship is for
If you can't work this equation then
I guess I'll have to show you the door
There is no need to say you love me
It would be better left unsaid

Say you'll be there
I'm giving you everything
All that joy can bring
this I swear

And all that I want from you is
a promise you will be there
Yeah I want you

Any fool can see they're falling
Gotta make you understand

I'll give you everything, on this I swear
Just promise you'll always be there

Say you'll be there
I'm giving you everything
All that joy can bring
this I swear

And all that I want from you is
a promise you will be there

WHAT'S THE STORY? "I think it means different things to each of us, but basically, it's saying that when you're in a relationship you should be there for each other, whether you're two girls or boy/girl. You don't have to give them all the 'I love you' bit, because what's important is if you're there for each other."

"We recorded it in our trakkies and socks in a studio in the producer's house. It was a cool vibe – dead laid-back. A lot of the sentiment in the song is to do with what we've been through together. We've always been there for each other, so we wrote about that."

say you'll be

SPECIAL BECAUSE... "The track was recorded in Elliot Kennedy's studio, which he actually named Spice, because it had never been used before."

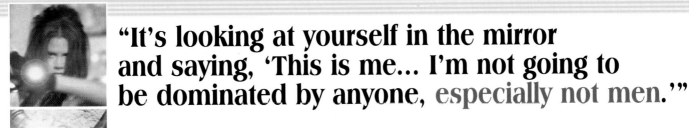

"It's looking at yourself in the mirror and saying, 'This is me... I'm not going to be dominated by anyone, especially not men.'"

ON VIDEO "This was one of my favourites. We were out in the desert and all getting on really well, so it was a complete laugh. It was very hot and I nearly got sunstroke! Two of the nights we went back to this hotel in the middle of nowhere – it was like Thelma and Louise." EMMA

"It was really friendly and vibey – the crew were great. I wore this neck thing in it and I really wanted it, but it belonged to the wardrobe. I had a three-stage plan to nick it, which involved me hiding it somewhere and someone else picking it up and hiding it, then someone else putting it in the car. It was really funny... One night Geri and I drove out into the desert. It was absolutely amazing. I sat on the car roof and gazed up at the stars. I felt so in touch with everything." MEL B

Director: Vaughn
Location: Los Angeles desert

"Geri sings, 'If you put two and two together, you will see what our friendship is for.' I immediately saw the $2+2=4$ pun in that and tried to explain it to the others, but they didn't get it at first. They're no good at maths!" VICTORIA

there

SPICE GIRLS
"2 BECOME 1" **VERSION 3**

DUR:3 MINS 56 SECS
DIR: BIG TV!
PROD:GARETH FRANCIS

VIRGIN RECORDS LTD.
20/11/96 STEREO

66 Old Compton St
London W1V 5PA
T 0171 437 8676
F 0171 734 3519

SPECIAL BECAUSE...
"It's basically a love song, but it's got a message – make sure you put a condom on if you're going to have sex. We all think that's very important." MEL **B**

"I have a Japanese tattoo on my stomach which means 'spirit, heart and mind.'"

Candle light and soul forever
A dream of you and me together
Say you believe it,
say you believe it
Free your mind
of doubt and danger
Be for real don't be a stranger
We can achieve it,
we can achieve it
Come a little bit closer baby,
get it on, get it on
'Cause tonight is the night
when two become one

I need some love that
I never needed love before
(Wanna make love to ya baby)
I had a little love,
now I'm back for more
(Wanna make love to ya baby)
Set your spirit free,
it's the only way to be

Silly games that you were playing,
empty words we both were saying
Let's work it out boy,
let's work it out boy
Any deal that we endeavour
Boys and girls feel good together
Take it or leave it,
take it or leave it

Are you as good
as I remember baby
Get it on, get it on
Cause tonight is the night
when two become one

I need some love that
I never needed love before
(Wanna make love to ya baby)
I had a little love,
now I'm back for more
(Wanna make love to ya baby)

Set your spirit free it's the only

Be a little bit wiser baby,
put it on, put it on
Cause tonight is the night
when two become one

I need some love that
I never needed love before
(Wanna make love to ya baby)
I had a little love,
now I'm back for more
(Wanna make love to ya baby)
I need some love that
I never needed love before
(Wanna make love to ya baby)
I had a little love,
now I'm back for more
(Wanna make love to ya baby)
Set your spirit free,
it's the only way to be

It's the only way to be

ON VIDEO
"I think this was my favourite video. My coat was wicked in it and it was really different to the other videos – shot entirely in the studio with high technology and loads of effects. It was really weird having to sing passionately into the camera – I was feeling a right mug in front of all those people singing 'Wanna make love to you baby'." VICTORIA

"This was definitely one of my favourite videos. They shot close up on facial expressions and it was very sexy. It's quite nice to act – I always look at the camera and think of someone I fancy and give it my all." EMMA

Director: Big TV   Location: A studio in South East London

"We had to be quiet when the deer comes in, right at the end of the video. So all day we were making deer jokes. Oh deer!" MEL B

two become one

WHAT'S THE STORY? "When we write it always reflects the kind of vibe we're on. Sometimes we're not in the mood to write uptempo jolly party songs and we all sit down to write a nice slow song. So one day we got together and started writing and the lyrics were getting a bit too slushy. We thought, hang on a minute, this isn't right. So we decided to include a safe sex message – 'Be a little bit wiser, baby – get it on, get it on'."

way to be

ON VIDEO  "Every video has a change of vibe, and this was another side to Spice. It was a nice cosy video. You do get a bit self-conscious singing straight at the camera, but you have to get over that, really." GERI

"I feel alive when I do mad things."

LOVE THING

You know I don't wanna know,
don't wanna know about that love thing
You know what I'm dreaming of
Don't wanna know about that love thing

Been broken hearted before
but that's the last time it happens to me
I keep on giving still you're asking for more
Too much emotion baby why can't you see
I'm not afraid of you love
Why can't you see I've had my share of that
You're what I want boy
You know you got boy
You gotta want me
It's just what I need
I'm not that easy as a matter of fact
There's no room for lovin'
stop that push and shovin', yeah
Don't wanna know about that love thing
Give me what I'm needing
you know what I'm dreaming of
Don't wanna know about that love thing

WHAT'S THE STORY?

"We wrote this the day after we left our first manager."

"The day after we walked out, we were meant to be working with a producer called Elliot Kennedy, who was going to help us write some songs. But because our management had arranged it, we didn't know where to find him or if he would still want to work with us. All we knew was that he was in Sheffield. So Geri and I drove all the way up there to look for him."

Now don't go wasting my time
You're not the only thing I've got on my mind
My friends are with me
when you ain't been around
Your precious words and promises
ain't bringing me down

I've got some living to do, don't assume I'm gonna be with you

"Eventually we found him and went to meet him in the middle of the night at someone's house. He must have thought we were mad, but it was worth it because he agreed to work with us."

You gotta want boy
You know you got boy
You gotta want me
It's just what I need
I'm not that easy as a matter of fact
There's no room for lovin',
stop that push and shovin' yeah
Don't wanna know about that love thing
Give me what I'm needing
You know what I'm dreaming of
Don't wanna know about that love thing

SPECIAL BECAUSE...

"Geri went missing on the morning we were meant to be going to the studio. When she got back, she said she'd just been for a walk. We got to the studio and started putting down the track and then she said: 'I've got a present **MEL B** for you all,' and went bright red and gave us a Spice ring each. We still wear them."

"I thought **G** they might all go 'You sad idiot'!"

V "When I sing this, I always think about how I was engaged before I got together with the girls. When I met them, I realised that it was all a mistake."

E "I also had a boyfriend and they helped me get rid of him."

MEL C "I was in a pretty bad relationship as well, and he went out the window. We helped each other out to get what we wanted and we gave each other strength."

MEL B "What we're saying is that you can't be anything else but what you are. That's how we got the best out of each other, by showing our hardcore nastiness, sadness and niceness – and that's when you know that you truly know someone – after you've seen every side of them. That's what's kept us so tight."

Stop pushing
You're rushing
You're losing my loving
I hope it
I'll see it
Just play it
You feel it
Gotta be bold, bold and oh so strong
Get with this and you got it goin' on
On and on with the girls named Spice

You wanna get with us
then you'd better think twice
God help the mister
yeah God help the mister
that comes between me and my sisters
I'm not afraid of your love
I'm not afraid of your love
Why can't you see I've had my share of that
You're what I want boy
You know you got boy
You've gotta want me
It's just what I need
I'm not that easy as a matter of fact
There's no room for lovin',
stop that push and shovin' yeah
Give me what I'm needing
You know what I'm dreaming of
Don't wanna know about that love thing

LAST TIME LOVER

WHAT'S THE STORY?

"It's about how boys gossip saying, 'Oh yeah, I had her last night and she did this and that.' Well, we did our version of it. It's stuffed with innuendoes. It means, I've been chasing this guy and 'His resistance was persistent' – as in, he kept on trying to get my knickers down. It goes on to say 'but I'm choosy, not a floozy' – basically that I had him, he wasn't any good and I want something better. So he was my 'last time lover', but he was 'lovin' under cover'." **MEL B**

"It's saying, I'm not a floozy – I like choosing the right men!" **E**

"Initially, we called it 'First Time Lover', and wrote it about losing your virginity. But we knocked that out." **G**

SPECIAL BECAUSE…

"We had a right laugh when we wrote it!" **MEL B**

Treat me right, all night
Make me feel good like you should

Listen up I gotta tell ya
About the ins and outs and goings on
I wouldn't tell just anybody
about the fox that I've been chasing
He's resistant not persistant,
it didn't stop me from homing in
Cos I'm choosy not a floozy,
I get my hit and then I run with it

Last time lover
Do you think I'm really cool and sexy,
and I know
you want to get with me
Last time lover
Do you wanna be my last time baby
Could it be your first time maybe
We got up and down to it,
like the dirty bass in the music
I got my major chords strummin'
took some time,
and then we're really buzzin'
First bite whet my appetite,
second helping's always better
Started getting burning hot,
I found my pride not easy
Slowed it down I said stop

Last time lover
Do you think I'm really cool and sexy,
and I know you want to get with me
Last time lover
Do you wanna be my last time baby
Could it be your first time maybe
Last time lover, treat me right
Lovin' under cover, all night
Last time lover, makes me feel good
Lovin' under cover like you should
Last time lover
Last time lover, treat me right
Lovin' under cover all night

Cool sexy, ever ready, someone fine,
always steady, gentle hands, dirty mind
Use your head and don't be blind
Words of love they don't wash with me,
what's the rush no urgency you see
Crazy boy, potential lover,

First and last lover brother there ain't no other

Crazy, sweety, cool but racy,
steady ready go, yes

Last time lover
Do you think I'm really cool and sexy,
and I know you want to get with me
Last time lover
Do you wanna be my last time baby,
could it be your first time maybe
Last time lover, treat me right,
lovin' under cover
Last time lover, make me feel good,
lovin' under cover like you should
Last time lover, treat me right,
lovin' under cover all night

SOMETHING KINDA FUNNY

We've got something kinda funny going on
We've got something kinda funny going on

Wherever you're going, high or low
Remember to sure enjoy the show
So climb aboard my journey deep inside
Better late than dead on time
Ooh, it's you I know
that I have got to feed
Ooh, don't take from me
More than you really need
More than you really need

We've got something kinda funny going on
We've got something kinda funny going on

Happiness is just a state of mind
Keep searching
Who knows what you may find

Rules are for fools

and fool's paradise is hard to find
Play my game or get left behind
It's you I know that
I have got to feed
Take from me
what you feel that you need
You feel that you need

We've got something kinda funny going on
We've got something kinda funny going on

You've got it…
Feelin' kinda funny,
when I'm with you honey
Feeling kinda queasy,
I ain't that easy

We've got something kinda funny

WHAT'S THE STORY?

"It's about how there must have been 'something kinda funny' going on with us lot, and how it was fate that we all met up."

SPECIAL BECAUSE…

"It was the first song that our manager heard, a few months before we finally signed with him."

mama

WHAT'S THE STORY? "It's all about how you're such a cow to your mum when you're going through that rebellious teenage stage. Then, when you get a bit older, you realise that whatever she was doing, she was only doing it for your own good and you think, 'Shit, I was really horrible!'."

"We wrote it when I was going through a bad phase with my mum. The sentiments are really that your mum's probably the best friend you've got. Whether she's a bit of a landmine or just over-protective, she probably knows you better than you know yourself."

"Mama is dedicated to our mothers."

ON VIDEO "It took a long time to film it, but it was nice that our mums were there and could see what we're doing. They were actually knackered at the end of the day and I said to my mum, 'Ha! Now you know how I feel every day!'"
VICTORIA

"Another excellent video. It was really good for our mums to see what we do – all the waiting around and getting ready. Now they realise how tiring our work is! It was nice to have them there – and all the fans as well – so it was a really good vibe."
MEL C

Director: Big TV
Location: a studio in Ealing

"It was a bit much. I had to think about the video, make sure I looked good, pay attention to the fans and look after my mum – all at the same time!"

MAMA / who do you think you are

SPICE GIRLS

She used to be my only enemy
and never let me free
Catching me in places
that I knew I shouldn't be
Every other day
I crossed the line
I didn't mean to be so bad
I never thought you would
Become the friend I never had

Back then I didn't know why
Why you were misunderstood
So now I see through your eyes
All that you did was love
Mama I love you, Mama I care
Mama I love you, Mama my friend
My friend

I didn't want to hear it then but
I'm not ashamed to say it now
Every little thing
You said and did was right for me
I had a lot of time to think about
About the way I used to be
Never had a sense of my responsibility

Back then I didn't know why
Why you were misunderstood

So now I see through your eyes
All I can give you is love

Mama I love you, Mama I care
Mama I love you, Mama my friend
My friend

But now I'm sure I know why
Why you were misunderstood
So now I see through your eyes
All I can give you is love
Mama I love you, Mama I care
Mama I love you, Mama my friend
My friend

Mama I love you, Mama I care
Mama I love you, Mama my friend
My friend

G "Personally I found it a bit weird bringing my mum to work with me. If you worked in Sainsbury's, you wouldn't get your mum to sit with you on the till. But it was nice for them to get made up, have their hair done and feel glamorous."

WHAT'S THE STORY? "The song's about a serious bighead, like some of the people we've met in this industry who just think: 'Yeah, I'm a superstar'. It's saying: 'Look, you've really lost the plot. What do you think you're doing? You're so  caught up in this celebrity world.' We wrote it without thinking of ourselves and the irony of it."

ON VIDEO "We shot it at a really mad club – a real dive. The bogs were horrible and we had to have our make-up done in a Winnebago. The vibe was excellent, though – I think it was my favourite video because it was such good fun. I felt like a proper pop star again because we did these individual bits with a guy with a SteadyCam and we had to give it loads as we sang to the camera. It was just how you imagine it when you're young. We were all dressed up, too. I had a dress and shoes on for the first time ever and I felt like Kylie Minogue. There were loads of freaky extras – jugglers and fire eaters and weirdo people. It's just real party people." **MEL C**

Director: Greg Masurak   Location: A theatre in North London

WHO DO YOU THINK YOU ARE / mama
SPICE GIRLS
THE NEW COMIC RELIEF SINGLE FOR RED NOSE DAY '97

MEL C "It was a laugh more than anything. It's a giggle, a real party track."

SPECIAL BECAUSE... "There's a serious note to it, but a fun **G** note as well."

who do you

"My talent is giving every person I come into contact with that little bit of MEL C zest for life again. Life in general is f*ing hard."**

"The girls we worked with were so funny. It was fun being in front of the E camera. I had a bit of a nightmare with my clothes, but it worked out in the end. What I wanted to wear all went wrong, so I ended up in a fitted, long dress and I don't usually wear anything like that. I was proved wrong, though, and in the end it did look great."

The race is on to get out of the bottom
The top is high so your roots are forgotten
Giving is good as long as you're getting
What's driving you it's ambition and betting
I said who do you think you are?
Some kind of superstar
You've got to swing it, shake it, move it, make it
Who do you think you are?
Trust it, use it, prove it, groove it
Show me how good you are

You've got to swing it, shake it, move it, make it

Who do you think you are?
Trust it, use it, prove it, groove it
Show me how good you are

You're swelling out in the wrong direction
You've got the bug superstar you've been bitten
Your trumpet's blowing for far too long
Playing the snake of the ladder, but you're wrong

I said who do you think you are?
Some kind of superstar
You've got to swing it, shake it, move it, make it
Who do you think you are?
Trust it, use it, prove it, groove it
Show me how good you are
You've got to swing it, shake it, move it, make it
Who do you think you are?
Trust it, use it, prove it, groove it
Show me how good you are

You have got to reach on up, never lose your soul
You have got to reach on up, never lose control

I said who do you think you are?
Some kind of superstar
You've got to swing it, shake it, move it, make it
Who do you think you are?
Trust it, use it, prove it, groove it
Show me how good you are
You've got to swing it, shake it, move it, make it
Who do you think you are?
Trust it, use it, prove it, groove it
Show me how good you are

Swing it, shake it, move it, make it
Trust it, use it, prove it, groove it

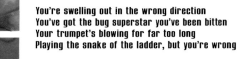

"I can honestly say I used to get more men interested in me before this. What's going on, good-looking men? Come on!"

think you are!

NAKED

Naivety and childhood left behind
deprived of the goodness of mankind
Past encounters have made her strong
strong enough to carry on and on

Undress her with your eyes,
uncover the truth from the lies
Strip you down don't need to care
lights are low exposed and bare

Naked
Nothing but a smile upon her face
Naked
She wants to play seek and hide,
no one to hide behind
Naked
The child has fallen from grace
Naked
Don't be afraid to stare
She is only naked

Naked
She knows exactly
what to do with men like you
Inside out in her mind there's
no doubt where you're coming from
Mystery will turn you on

Naked
Nothing but a smile upon her face
Naked
She wants to play seek and hide,
no one to hide behind
Naked
The child has fallen from grace
Naked
Don't be afraid to stare
She is only naked

Hello...

This angel's dirty face is sore,
holding on to what she had before
Not sharing secrets
with any old fool,
now she's gonna keep her cool
She wants to get naked
She wants to get naked

Naked
Nothing but a smile upon her face
Naked
She wants to play seek and hide,
no one to hide behind
Naked
The child has fallen from grace
Naked
Don't be afraid to stare
She is only naked

WHAT'S THE STORY?

"It's a weird track, which we recorded in Absolute Studios. We were thinking about what it's like when you walk into a room and everybody stops and looks, as though you've got no clothes on. We've all had that in one way or another." **MEL B**

"It's also about how when you have a relationship and you start to bare your soul – then you wanna hold back, because you've opened up too soon." **E**

SPECIAL BECAUSE...

"It's called 'Naked', but it's not necessarily about getting naked. It's more about baring your soul and feeling exposed." **V**

IF YOU CAN'T DANCE

If you can't dance, if you can't dance
If you can't dance, if you can't dance
If you can't dance to this you can't do
Nothing for me baby
If you can't dance, if you can't dance
If you can't dance, if you can't dance
If you can't dance to this you can't do
Nothing for me baby

Now we got the flavour,
the bad behaviour
The rhythm, the melody,
the juice for you to savour
rockin' and vibing somebody is jivin'
You need to take a tip, sort it out
Get a grip whenever I go out
wherever it may be
There is never a Keanu
but a dweeb lookin' at me
But then even if I did score
He's a loser on the dance floor
Take a deep breath count 1, 2, 3

Even when his eyes met mine
His slamming moves were out of time
Can't you just feel the groove why don't
You move it's easy can't you see
Take my hands and dance with me

If you can't dance, if you can't dance
If you can't dance, if you can't dance
If you can't dance to this you can't do
Nothing for me baby
If you can't dance, if you can't dance
If you can't dance, if you can't dance
If you can't dance to this you can't do
Nothing for me baby

If you can't dance, if you can't dance
If you can't dance, if you can't dance
If you can't dance to this you can't do
Nothing for me baby
If you can't dance, if you can't dance
If you can't dance, if you can't dance
If you can't dance to this you can't do
Nothing for me baby

SPECIAL BECAUSE...

"It's about having preconceptions about people. **G** Someone might look a certain way, but when you meet them they're completely the opposite of what you expected."

WHAT'S THE STORY?

V "This one's about when you go to a club and you see a really good-looking bloke who seems really nice, and then you go to dance and it's 'Oh, no! What's going on?'"

MEL C "I love the lyric 'there is never a Keanu but a dweeb'. You get these ugly blokes who'll go up to anyone!"

SPICE GIRLS

1. wannabe
2.52

2. say you'll be there
3.56

3. 2 become 1
4.00

4. love thing
3.37

5. last time lover
4.11

6. mama
5.03

7. who do you think you are
3.59

8. something kinda funny
4.02

9. naked
4.26

10. if u can't dance
3.50

Management: Simon Fuller at 19 Management Ltd

GIRLS on GIRLS

"We fall out all the time – it's only natural – but since we've been together and got to know each other better, we're getting on better than ever before. Because of what we're doing, we're under quite a lot of stress, so we've got to stick togther, and we do.

We really care about each other

and want the best out of each other, so we all look after each other. We've all grown up. We've had to mature, because we've done a lot of travelling, seen a lot of the world, had a lot of shit thrown at us and met a lot of people you've got to be wary of. We haven't changed as people – we've kept our original personalities. People expect you to change, but you don't. It's everyone else who changes."

MEL C

	on Victoria	on Geri	on Mel C	on Mel B	on Emma
Victoria		"When I first met her, I thought, 'Who is this nutter in mad clothes?' Now I'm used to it, she just seems really normal to me. Every time she used to say something, I used to feel a bit scared to say anything back, but now I just shut her up if I want to."	"She's come out of herself. She's not as quiet as she used to be. That's the main difference."	"She's not as irrational any more. She just used to say something without thinking about the consequences, but now she won't do that."	"She's a lot more grown up now, but she's still a baby in the sense that she needs lots of attention and cuddles and things like that."
Geri	"She's become a lot more independent and she's grown. She's got a lot more attitude about her now. She's always had it in her, but now she's a lot more expressive, which is good."		"She's really blossomed into a babe!"	"She's matured and chilled out a little bit now. She's a lot more relaxed and laid-back."	"She's really, really grown. I think you change a lot between eighteen and twenty-one and she's really matured."
Mel C	"She's not posh! She might wear posh clothes, but she's just as common as the rest of us!"	"She's always been the bossy bigmouth – and she's still the same! No change there."		"She's just the same – the mad, energetic one who never sits still. Big mouth, big hair – at least she's matching!"	"Even though she's 21 now, she's still our baby because she's the youngest. Sometimes, though, you'd think she was the eldest because she shouts at us and tells us we're being silly."
Mel B	"I now know she has the same sick, perverse humour as me. She's great."	"I still think she's a nutter. She hasn't changed!"	"She's still the most disciplined and the strongest in spirit and determination. She never panics."		"I would have thought that she was all sweet and innocent, but she's not really. She just likes having a laugh and takes the piss out of herself and everyone."
Emma	"Vicky's cool. We chat all the time on the phone. I'm always ring her for advice on what to wear. I like going out with her because she goes to posh places! When you catch her on a funny day, you won't stop laughing. She's got a really dry sense of humour."	"Geri's a bit mad, but she's really good when you want advice about something or want a shoulder to cry on. We went out partying in Dublin the other day and she and I were the only ones who stayed up. We're not usually the party animals, but really, deep down, maybe we are!"	"She's my bubby. We drive to work together because we live nearby and I see her a lot at weekends. I can truly say I would trust her with my life. She's a babe. My friends all fancy the others, but they fall in love with Melanie C!"	"She's brilliant as well. I love chatting to her. I go round to her house quite a lot. We just sit and talk about crap, really. That's what I like about her – it doesn't have to be anything important. But I haven't been out partying with her for a while – I think she's slowing down!"	

49

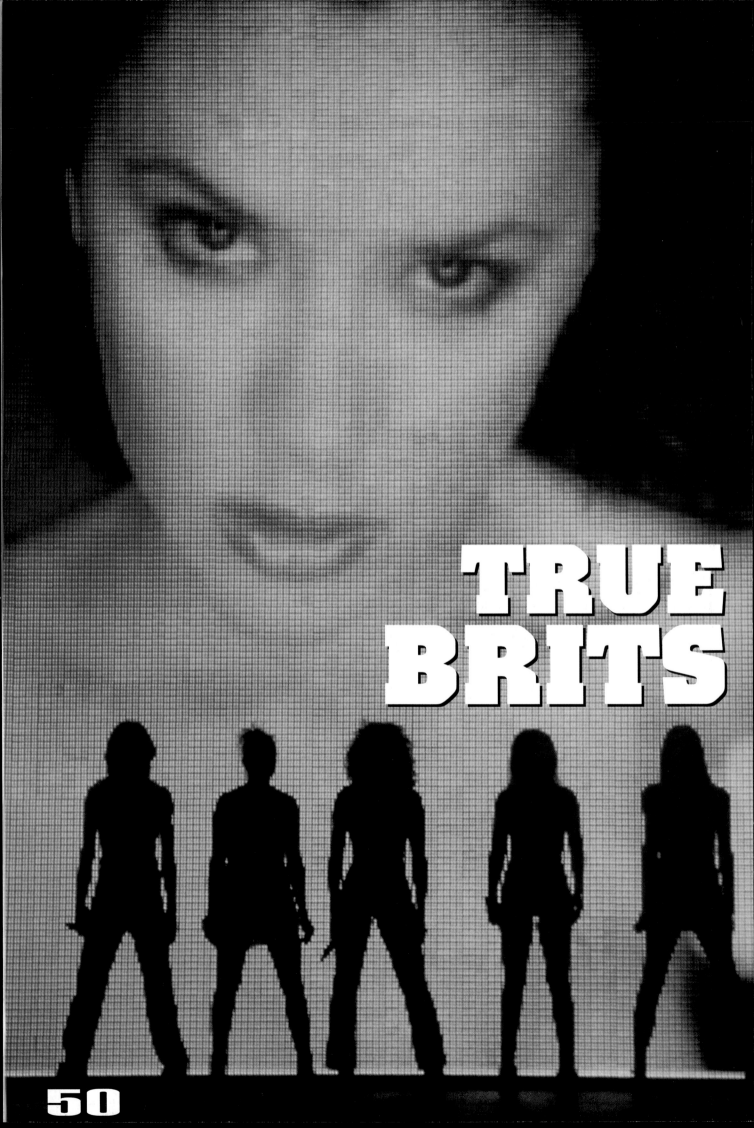

TRUE
BRITS

SPICES COMING HOME!
24 FEB 1997
BEHIND-THE-SCENES ON A NIGHT OF TRIUMPH FOR GIRL POWER

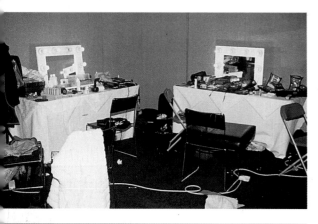

Victoria

"We've had some really rough times, and when we do taste the high life, when we hear kids screaming, we really appreciate it."

"I'm a worrier, a bag of nervous energy. That's why I'm tired all the time. I just can't lie in bed. When we haven't got anything to do the rest of the girls will be in bed until four in the afternoon, but not me. I'm up at seven with a big list of things to do. My anxious personality won't let me relax.

"I'd like to be able to try and slow down, but there's no chance of that at the minute. Everything's just too hectic. I love what I do though, even if some people think I look miserable in photos because I don't smile much. That's not looking miserable, that's me trying not to look too cheesy. I'm just not as upfront as Geri and Mel B. People asked me why I was in the background on the 'Wannabe' video, but it just wouldn't be in my nature to be running across the screen screaming 'I'll tell you what I want' at the top of my lungs.

"The whole thing about being famous and everyone wanting to be nice to you and be your friend is a bit alien to me, because I was never popular when I was at school. I was never physically bullied, but I was definitely given a hard time mentally. I never drank, smoked or swore at the teachers, so I suppose people didn't think I was very cool. I never had loads of

Favourite word?
bollocks
It's so expressive

55

friends and that was quite sad, but I had to grin and bear it. The newspapers made a really big deal of my loneliness, but it was never that bad, and at least it taught me that being the most popular girl in school isn't the most important thing in the world.

"When I moved on to dancing school I was told that my legs weren't long enough, my hair wasn't right and a load of other things should be better. I was never chosen for anything, but now I have the headmistress ringing me up going 'Oh darling, you must come in to college sometime.' I think I'll go there one day and just give it to them big-time, tell all the girls that it doesn't matter if they're short or fat or whatever.

"Nowadays I'm amazed that I have photographers chasing me about. I came out of my place the other day and got in my car which was in the car park. There were all these people with long lenses hanging about and pointing their cameras and I thought to myself 'What are they taking pictures of the trees for?' Then I realised it was me they were shooting! My boyfriend was in a fashion show the other week and I turned up

to watch him and all the photographers wanted was shots of me. I was really embarrassed for him.

"I don't know why the papers seem to want me so much. I'm supposedly the posh one, though I don't know if that's the reason why. Anyway, I'm far from posh. I don't talk posh and I don't think of myself as posh. I do like designer clothes, I suppose, and at least my mum was happy when she found out that was my nickname. Do the others take the piss out of my nickname? Not when they're called Scary Spice and Baby Spice, they don't!

"I don't think of myself as someone who people look up to. I think the band as a whole is a role model, but not me as a person, because each of us has a different kind of fan and the younger fans don't seem to go for me. I try not to think too hard about other people's views. If I want to wear a tiny skirt and a bikini top then I'm doing it for me, not for any men who are watching.

"The performance side is only part of what Spice Girls is about anyway. I really enjoy working with the other girls in the studio;

"We're not claiming to be soul divas, we're just having a laugh."

"Wherever you go now, it's like walking into the room with no clothes on – people start staring at you. It's a bit of a shock. We've been travelling so much we haven't read the papers, haven't watched much television, haven't been listening to the radio, because we haven't got time.

So we're not seeing ourselves in the same way as everybody else."

"If we want to get drunk or eat loads of cream cakes then we do. We want young girls at school to relate to us, to be one of us. Kids can smell bullshit. We want to be positive role models for young girls and women."

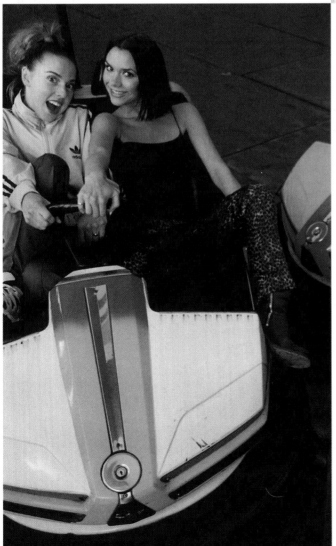

✓ Best advice:
What to do.
My mum taught me the facts of life, although I think I told her more than she told me, in the end!

✗ Worst advice:
Do it like a lady!

BEST CHAT-UP LINE:
"I like your clothes. They'd look really
good on my bedroom floor."

WORST CHAT-UP LINE:
"How much does a polar bear weigh?
I don't know, but it breaks the ice."

sitting around, chatting, vibeing off
each other. I'd like to play some
instruments better. I've tried to learn
the piano a million times, but I've got
a really short attention span. I
haven't even sat and watched telly for
over two years, because I don't have
the patience to sit through a whole
programme.
"I really enjoy my life, but I've had
to re-adjust to living a different way.

I have to look for different pleasures.
Whenever I've been away and finally
get back home it takes me at least a
day and a half to get back to normal.
And you know what I really enjoyed
the other day? Getting in my car and
going to the newsagents without being
photographed. I was screaming 'Spin
on this' on my way back and sticking
my finger in the air. People must have
thought I was mad!" V

THE FIRST TIME I...

...bought a record
It was something from Buck's Fizz. My worst record is the B52's 'Love Shack'. I tell you, if I saw the B52's, I'd get Mel to kick them in the face!

...got in trouble
I never, ever get in trouble. I'm always really good. Even as a child, I was really boring and really good. But I tell you what I did do once – my dad bought a brand new van and we'd just had a brand new wall built. Me and my brother and sister got in the van and I knocked the handbrake off, so it rolled down the drive and smashed the brick wall in. Brand new van, brand new brick wall – my dad went absolutely ballistic. And I blamed it all on my little brother!

...saw a film more than once
I watched 'Grease' over and over again. I used to think I was actually Sandy. I wanted some tight satin trousers and some high-heeled shoes, but my mum wouldn't let me. Then my mum's friend promised she'd get me some and she never did. Now you should never promise something to a kid when you're not going to deliver, because I haven't forgotten to this day. In my mind she still owes me some satin trousers!

...lied and got caught out
I never get caught.

...appeared on stage
I did some shows when I was very young – two or three. When I was about eight I did one where I was dressed up in a bright yellow top hat and tails with sequins all over it, yellow fishnet tights and yellow tap shoes with yellow bows. I tap danced to 'If My Friends Could See Me Now', that Shirley Maclaine song from 'Sweet Charity' – and I was Shirley Maclaine.

...wore make-up
I came out with a full face on, I think! No, the first make-up I ever wore was when I was about thirteen. It was bright blue eyeliner and I thought I was really cool.

...stayed out all night
I was going to clubs when I was about fourteen. Not very credible clubs, I'd like to add – tacky ones, in fact. I had a good relationship with my mum and dad – they never minded picking me up at about 3 or 4 in the morning.

...fancied a pop star
Matt Goss was the first. I was going to marry him. At some point the novelty wore off though.

...went to a football match
In February, I went to see Manchester United v Chelsea and I got really into it. Mel told me the rules about where you had to score goals and stuff. I went with the flow and followed the little players by the numbers on their backs and who had the best legs. They were all wearing rather unflattering shorts, though – they need at least five inches cut off the bottom – and they'd look a lot better if they pulled their socks down.

...saw a live concert
'The Kids from Fame' – they were really good.

...went abroad
I've been on holiday every year since I was born – to the Canary Islands and Spain.

...had a near-death experience
It was a really hot day. I was in my Brownie uniform and I'd just got my safety in the home badge. You know when you really need a drink and you don't just sip it, you glug it down without tasting it. Well, I saw a mug of liquid on the side and drank the whole thing before I realised that it was a cup of pure bleach. Suddenly, I couldn't breathe. I ran out to the garden where my mum was. "Stop being so rude, I'm talking to the gardener!" she said as I was gasping away. She thought I was joking! Then she realised and the gardener held me up by my feet and shook me up and down to try and make me throw up, which is actually the worst thing to do, because it just brings the burning sensation back up. Finally mum took me to hospital and it all turned out okay.

...wore a mini skirt
I had hotpants which I wore out clubbing when I was about fourteen. I also had a big, terrible perm. I thought people were looking at me because I was so cool, but they were probably thinking, "What a mug!"

...killed an animal
I used to collect worms and lay them out on a slate, chop them up and watch them go their separate ways. Then I'd put all the bits in a jam jar.

...got drunk
My mum and dad have always been quite Spanish about alcohol – there's always wine on the table. I never got totally pissed when I was younger, but recently I did. My sister brought me home and I fell out of the car! I felt rough like a chainsaw the next day. We had to do a shoot in a hot air balloon for a TV show at five o'clock in the morning and I had a hangover from hell! It was a nightmare. It was really cold and damp and early and we had to lie on the ground and be pulled up by the balloon. I was lying there with a pair of Gucci shoes on thinking, "It's five o'clock in the morning. It's freezing cold. I've got a nice new pair of shoes and a nice suit on and I'm lying in some shitty field where cows have dunged everywhere. This is not rock and roll! I couldn't see Liam and Noel doing this." I wasn't impressed.

...won a prize
I used to win dancing competitions all the time. At school at lunchtime, no-one got a break because they all had to sit in the classroom and watch me dancing. I always won the prizes. I had the main part in the show, or I wouldn't be in it. One year I didn't get the main part and I said: "That's such a shame because my mum's got the perfect outfit for it." She didn't really, so when I got home I begged her to make me a snowman outfit so that I could have the main part!

...went to hospital
When I swallowed that bleach by mistake.

...went to school
I can't remember the first day. I always used to cry when the holidays ended. I hated school and I never wanted to go back.

...fell in love
I was only about seventeen when I got engaged and that was love. It isn't now – we split up! I'm glad I didn't marry him. And I've still got the ring – because I've got Girl Power!

...got an A
For art – that was the only thing I was any good at, really. I wasn't a straight-A's kind of student.

"There's no room for bitchiness in this group. We all lead in different areas. I'm still me even after all that's happened. If my family told me I'd changed I'd be in big, big trouble, but they don't. We never go to starry parties. If we want to go out, we go down the pub, or out for a meal with our mates."

Comic Relief '97

SPICE GIRLS V SUGAR LUMPS

MEL B

"Really, really good fun – the best! It was my kind of environment, full of freaky misfits who were loud and proud."

VICTORIA

"It was the most fun because Dawn French was playing me and she was really funny. We had a real laugh. We're going to go out with her one night, actually. She said, 'Come round my house for dinner,' and I said, 'But it'll be all girls, so Lenny can't come'. She said: 'I tell you what, I'll get Lenny to do the cooking.' I said okay and gave her all our food requirements and we're going to make it a date."

GERI

I enjoyed it so much – it was fantastic. The women were all really warm and funny and nice. The freakiest thing about it was seeing Jennifer Saunders. She looked just like me and everyone said they thought she was me. It was absolutely bizarre – the make-up, everything. It was scary – like, do I really do that? She takes on people and she'd got all my mannerisms exactly. It was the most in-yer-face – a reflection of me. And I was thinking, omigod!

WE ARE THE NEWS!

WHO WANNABE A MILLIONAIRE

By LENNY LOTTERY

THERE'S only one place you
Wannabe tonight — watching
the first ever midweek Lottery
draw on BBC1 at 8pm.
The Spice Girls have inter-
rupted their American tour to
join host Carol Smillie and star
guests for the Winsday show
with £10million up for grabs.
Last time the Fab Five sang
on Saturday's National Lottery

Live it notched up one of
highest audiences with alm
16 million viewers.
During the show, each Sp
Girl will talk about a pe
cause that has received c
from the Lottery.
So what do they really, re
ly want? To read all about
mid-week Lottery draw in
great eight-page pullout!

WHAT WILLS ROYALLY ROYALLY WANTS!

Top of the pin-ups... the Spice Girls with Emma second-left and, right, Emma in Baywatch costume

Spice Girl's his No1

EXCLUSIVE by JAMIE PYATT

PRINCE WILLIAM has dumped his Pamela
Anderson poster for a new bedside pin-up
— of Spice Girls stunner Emma Bunton.

Wills, 14, has torn down a 3ft picture of
Pam in her red Baywatch swimsuit at his
room at Eton College.

He has replaced it with a dazzling poster of his
latest dreamboat Emma,
20, youngest in the sexy
all-girl band.

Wills is a huge fan of
the group, whose Nol
hit Wannabe had the
catchy line Tell Me
What You Want, What
You Really Really Want.

He snapped up their
album after popping into
his local Our Price
record store yards from
Windsor Castle.

The Prince, who was
with his detective and
several Eton pals, paid
£12.99 for the girls' CD
called Spice.

Costumes

At the same time he
picked up the poster of
blonde Emma — then
rushed back to Eton to
put it on his wall.

Our last week The
Sun featured an exclu-
sive photo of Emma and
her four pals sporting
Pam-style red cos-
tumes on a California
beach.

An Eton source said:
"The Spice Girls are the
big group with all the
boys at the moment.

"They argue over
which girl is sexiest but
Wills has the hots for
Emma Bunton. It's a
normal schoolboy crush.

and he is head over
heels. He has consigned
Pam's poster to the
wastepaper basket.

"And he has already
asked his mum if he can
see the Spice Girls in
concert."

An Our Price spokes-
man said: "We get all
the Eton boys in here
and Prince William got
no special treatment.

"But he has great
taste — Emma is the
prettiest of the bunch."

Besides Emma the
Spice Girls are Geri
Halliwell, 24, Melanie
Brown, 21, Victoria Ad-
ams, 21, and Melanie
Chisholm...

SAVE £200
BEST DIGITAL DEAL

FREE 3 MONTHS LINE RENTAL
WORTH £25.38 inc VAT

FREE 10 MINS OF CALLS PER
MONTH FOR FIRST 3
MONTHS up to £61.89p*
THREE AFTER

FREE 75 MINS OF CALLS PER
MONTH FOREVER
(worth up to £19.88 a mnt)

FREE LEATHER CARRY CASE
WORTH UP TO £25.00

100 HOUR BATTERY

PER SECOND BILLING

FREE next day delivery

£9.99

NOKIA 1610
● 11 hours talk time
● Supplied with rapid mains charger
● 4hr level of security

Ref: VSV101 VODAFONE

Have your credit card to hand and
Dial-a-phone now on Freephone

0800 00 00 77
24 Hours DIAL-A-PHONE

---

what 's getting

ery has written to sexy model
ash her for sending him a bunch
osters of herself.

, 27 — a top pin-up girl in
ted the 12-year-old Prince after
t Cindy Crawford had a date in
der brother William.

oshe said yesterday: "I read that
and felt left out. So I sent him a
is note telling him I'd be
his pin-up girl.

"To my surprise, one
of Prince Charles' aides
wrote back saying he re-
ceived the posters and
was really grateful.

"I'll be his pen-pal,
which I'm sure will
please his mum because
I am a wholesome girl.

"He is such a hand-
some young man and I'm
dying to meet him."

Cindy

"When I was little I always thought I want
to be famous. But you could never drea
of what's happened to us. It's
a bit out of the ordinary."

"My mum always has
the latest magazines ready fo
me when I arrive home. She
keeps all our press cuttings
and sometimes buys two copie
of each magazine in case we'r
on both sides
of the page."

VOTE SPICE

● Major's a boring pillock-but better than the rest ●

● Blair's just a marketing man with no ideas ●

● The whole European federal plan is ridiculous ●

THE chart-topping Spice Girls
have declared their political col-
ours in an outspoken interview
in the high-brow weekly magazine, The Spectator.

The fab five, aged between 20
and 24, give their astonishing
frank views on Mr Major, Tony
Blair, Europe, Lady Thatcher,
family values and the Royal
Family. Their thoughts make
gripping reading.

SEE PAGES 4 & 5

Spicing up politics... the Spice Girls have firm views on Mr Major & Co

LABOUR IN

IT'S A GIRLS WORLD...

BIZARRE

SPICE GIRLS SPECIAL BY ANDY COULSON (He supports Spurs so Emma could be his perfect woman)

Kits out for the lads

MY Christmas has come early—The Spice Girls have got their kits out for the lads!

Britain's hottest pop group prove they're a winning team in the latest issue of football magazine 90 Minutes.

And the girls are on target for a spectacular score next week. Their new single 2 Become 1 was released yesterday and looks set to be No 1 over Christmas after staggering advance orders of 675,000 copies.

By the way girls, any chance of a football strip!

| MEL B | VICTORIA | GERI | MEL C | EMMA |

MEL B A Yorkshire lass, Mel B cheers on Leeds United.

Mel, 21, nicknamed Scary Spice, says: "I'm kind of into football but in a girlie way - I like looking at their legs and they way they get all sweaty and that...

"I went out with a footballer for a while. He was a trainee for Leeds but his career was cut short through injury. The best thing I like about it is the way the crowd connect. It's such a good vibe when you're all cheering your side together. I love that.

"I've met David Batty. I used to see him quite a lot. He was a bit of a lad. "Who's going to win the League? Ooh, I don't know. Liverpool? No, Leeds! I'm supposed to be a Leeds fan, me, dad'll go mad"

VICTORIA POSH Spice Victoria, 22, has no favourite team.

Victoria, from Goff's Oak, Herts, says "As my manager Simon supports Manchester United I thought I'd go for them. And I have heard that some of the fans are worth checking out!

"I don't know anything about football. If Jamie Redknapp came up and slapped me I wouldn't know who he was.

"Last year my parents had a party, a big marquee in the garden, and Sporty keeper Ian Walker along with some friends. "Everyone was loads except me — I didn't know who anyone was except one who was. We were all for a while but I wasn't paying any attention and haven't spoken to him

GERI GINGER Spice Geri, 24, supports her local team, second division Watford.

She says "I'm proud to represent the underdog. I'd like to say hello to their midfielder Cory Porter and gets tickets for me. But

MEL C SPORTY Spice Melanie Chisholm, 22, is a lifelong Liverpool fan. She says: "I got into Anfield for nothing now as rivals Arsenal and Tottenham.

"I met Steve McMananman after one of the games and gets tickets for me. But

EMMA BLONDE Spice Emma, 20, comes from Finchley, north London - the home of arch rivals Arsenal and Tottenham.

She says: "All my family are Spurs fans. My dad's girlfriend once bought

VOTE FOR THE BRATS! THE NME READER

NME
NEW MUSICAL EXPRESS

PUPPET
The roar power of TIGER

72

JUST SAY FERRINO! STEVE COOGAN'S latest bluff

SEX! SUCCESS! STREAKING! SHOPPING! TONY B

SPICE GIRLS

The ULTIMATE rock'n'roll inte

KISS • CATATONIA • SNOOP DOGGY DOGG
TINDERSTICKS • SKUNK ANANSIE • JAMIROQUAI

"It's like George Michael says, you can't go around trying to please everyone, because you end up diluting what you are all about."

"When it all started, you couldn't get your head around it. But now we realise you don't have to get your head around it."

THE SPICE GIRLSZZZZ

Pop beauties are really big snooze on Canadian tour

★ SNORE blimey! Two Spice Girls become one as they cuddle up to grab forty winks on a flight during their American promo tour.

The dream girls — Geri Halliwell, 24, and Victoria Adams, 22 — hit the recline button almost as soon as they sat in their first class

We're a dream team . . . Geri, left, and Victoria cuddle up during the flight

---

BABES MAKE FORTUNE AS DEBUT U.S. SINGLE HITS No1

THANKS A MILLION . . . the girls — from left, Mel C, Emma, Mel B, Victoria and Geri — can expect the cash to flood in after cracking the U.S. market   Picture: RETNA

FLAG-NIFICENT . . . Britain's pop sensations wrapped in the Union Jack and the Stars and Stripes

HOW SALES STACK UP

7.2m
2.6m

3.5m
5m

BIZARRE

ALL THE RESULTS IN FULL

THE 1996 READERS POLL AWARD WINNERS

WONNABE!
Spice Girls scoop top gongs

Best Group: SPICE GIRLS
Worst Group: ROBSON & JEROME
Best Single: WANNABE, SPICE GIRLS
Best Newcomer: SPICE GIRLS
Sexiest Female Star: GERI, SPICE GIRLS
Sexiest Male Star: LIAM GALLAGHER
Best Male Singer: RONAN KEATING, BOYZONE

TOP ALBUM ... George

Best Female Singer: LOUISE
Best Film Star: SLY STALLONE
Best Tour: BOYZONE
Best Album: OLDER, GEORGE MICHAEL
Best DJ: CHRIS EVANS
Top TV Personality: CHRIS EVANS
Top TV Show: EASTENDERS
Ugliest Star: LIAM GALLAGHER

BEST SINGER ... Ronan

Best Dressed Star: LIAM GALLAGHER
Worst Dressed Star: PAUL GASCOIGNE
Chris De Burgh Loathsome Achievement Award: PAUL GASCOIGNE
Worst TV Show: NEIGHBOURS

BAB FAB . . . telly's Barbara Windsor

SPICING ON THE CAKE . . . the girls join me to celebrate their poll triumph.   Pictures: DAVE HOGAN

THE Spice Girls have cleaned up in the most important awards of all — the 1996 Bizarre Reader's Poll.

Thousands of you voted for your favourite stars. Britain's sexiest band picked up four gongs - Best Group, Best Newcomer, Best Single (Wannabe) and Sexiest Female Star (Geri). Geri, Victoria, Mel B, Mel C and Emma - at No1 for Christmas - were stunned when I presented them with their awards at a top London hotel.

Emma said "It's fantastic. We can't

The Bizarre poll is important because it's the fans who are voting. This is the best Christmas present we could hope for."

Chris Evans was another big winner in the poll that counts. The controversial star was named Best DJ for his

Gorgeous Geri, left, was voted readers' hottest star

Radio 1 breakfast show AND Top TV Personality for TFI Friday.

Chris gave away two prizes he won at the Comedy Awards this month. He said "Usually I hate winning things but the Bizarre poll is different.

"It's an honour to know of many Sun readers like what I'm doing. Their opinion counts for an awful lot.

Proud

"I won't be giving these awards away."

Liam Gallagher picked up a hat-trick of honours, being named Sexiest AND Ugliest Male star. You also voted the Oasis singer Best Dressed Star (honest).

My old mate Paul Gascoigne is the proud owner of a Worst Dressed Star award and was also named - with

frightening predictability - Most Loathsome Star.

Louise was thrilled to be named Best Female Singer and said. "I'm absolutely delighted You know you're doing something right when you win a Bizarre award. Thank you to everyone who voted for me."

Boyzone- who swept the board at the recent Smash Hits awards - got two Bizarre prizes for Best Tour and Best Male Singer (Ronan Keating).

They sent their thanks from the Far East where they are on tour, saying "The Bizarre awards are the ones we look out for. Ronan's chuffed to bits and we are all pleased that you liked our live show so much."

Sly Stallone was stormed to be named Best Film Star. As I handed over the award when we met last week, the movie superstar said "The Sun is one of the biggest papers in the

---

"We want to be a household name. We want to be a Fairy Liquid or Ajax."

63

Spice Style

How we dress,
where we shop,
mistakes we've made
and what we'd like
to wear in our dreams!

Style: "It varies. Sort of Lenny Kravitz/Prince, hippy but not hippy... and outrageously tight." **Shops:** "I get a lot of stuff from Jean Paul Gaultier. He's got a mad, quite ethnic feel to his stuff. And any little bits and bats that look good – whether it be from Selfridges or Warehouse."

Mel B

Worst outfit: "A sequinned boob-tube with matching hot pants that my mum made me. I stood out like a right prat in it." **Fashion fantasy:** "I'd like to go completely Indian. I like that cultural stuff, like the Afro-Caribbean look, when they wear big turbans and traditional dress. I love dressing up like that."

Style: "I like being sporty and sometimes I like to be smart, but I always want to feel mobile, like I can do a backflip at any moment. Sometimes I wear smart hipster trousers and little tank tops, so you can see my tattoos. I may wear high heels for special occasions, but I'm usually in trainers." **Shops:** "We've been really lucky because we've been given loads of stuff. I've got some great Dolce &

Mel C

Gabbana clothes and there's a really good designer called Owen Gaster, who does very nice trousers. JD Sports is my favourite shop. French Connection and Morgan do some good stuff, too." **Worst outfit:** "When I was about fifteen, I thought I was really, really trendy wearing a pair of very badly ripped jeans. They were quite sad." **Fashion fantasy:** "To be able to wear skirts like Victoria (but I don't really like my legs)."

Style: "I quite like my short skirts and tight shirts – with big bovvers, but pretty little socks. If I go for a funky look I'll make it look prettier by wearing frilly socks or having my hair in pigtails. I don't like to look too hard or too sexy – I like to look quite cute, so it's not too in-yer-face. I used to try and hide my curves, but now I think, well I've got them and I may as well use them!" **Shops:** "I'm a massive Miss Selfridge fan and I love Top Shop, Kookaï and Karen Millen – wherever I feel comfortable. All the posh shops just cater for tall, skinny girls." **Worst outfit:** "It's disgusting – a bright yellow dress with butterflies all over it. I've still got it at home." **Fashion fantasy:** "I've always wanted to wear a very beautiful, long, fitted dress – and I did at the Brits. I loved it – it was so sexy. So hopefully I can start wearing more dresses like that now."

Emma

"None of us are conventional beauties. That's inspiring for girls because it shows you don't have to be gorgeous to be up there doing it!"

Style: "I really like glamorous clothes and I love Seventies coats and things like that. I've always been a bit different with what I wear – but not on purpose. It's just a reflection of who I am." **Shops:** "My sister makes a lot of my clothes. It's great because I'll draw her a picture of something I want and she'll turn it into reality. I also like market and old second-hand clothes. I always used to shop in Oxfam in Notting Hill Gate and Camden – that way, you get originals, rather than copies. I might get the odd little top from the high street, though." **Worst outfit:** "A really hideous puff-ball skirt." **Fashion fantasy:** "I really like getting into a character. My wardrobe's a fancy dress wardrobe – I dress however I feel that day."

Geri

Style: "I like being smart. I may wear tracksuit bottoms or jeans around the house, but I very rarely go out like that." **Shops:** "My favourite shop is Prada and I like Gucci and Plein Sud as well. I don't really ever go to high street stores." **Worst outfit:** "When I was about thirteen I had this outfit which I thought was really cool: a pair of salmon pink hotpants, black tights with a white map of the world on them, a blouse and big boots. Terrible!" **Fashion fantasy:** "A big ballgown – something like Princess Di's wedding dress."

Victoria

"We feel passionate about everything!"

"I've always been an independent girl, as long as I can remember. My mum used to work, so I was left to entertain myself a lot of the time. I'd even put my own bunches in my hair, then get myself off to school in the morning. Relying on myself made me the way I am today, living on my wits.

"I've always thought of myself as The Artful Dodger out of 'Oliver', blagging my way through life. I was managing to talk my way into clubs long before I was in the band and I suppose I sort of talked my way into Spice Girls too. I'm not a trained singer or dancer, but I knew that I could bring some spirit to the group, some Girl Power. I hope what I've managed to achieve now

Geri

"I'd like to be remembered as a wild freedom-fighter with method in her madness. Life itself is a lesson."

helps other women learn the lesson that they can do as much as anybody. When someone says I can't do something I derive energy from it and that fuels me even more to prove them wrong. I'm an expressive person, very outspoken, I feel like a freedom-fighter trying to give girls the right to express themselves.

"Sometimes other girls don't appreciate that. Mel C and I were at a Blur concert in London not too long ago and they put the spotlight on us. We waved and the whole place waved back, except for one girl who stuck two fingers up at me. I thought 'Where's your Girl Power?' I dunno. Maybe she was just drunk. Or maybe she didn't think doing nude photos like I did before I joined the band

Favourite word? **EXISTENTIALISM** · I don't know what it means, though.

✔ Best advice:
Follow your gut instinct and never believe what you read in the tabloids.
✘ Worst advice:
You can't do that.
Oh yes I can. I went to an all-girls school and was always being told off for wearing short skirts and eyeliner. I hated it.

THE FIRST TIME I...

...bought a record
It was 'Dancing Queen' by Abba. And the first record I snogged to was 'Move Closer'.

...got in trouble
When I was born! Actually, I remember one time that I climbed out of my bedroom window when I wasn't meant to be going out. When I was sneaking back in, my mum caught me and pulled me in by the hair. I was in big trouble then.

...saw a film more than once
'The Wizard of Oz'.

...lied and got caught out
When I said I was 5ft 7ins to a model agency!

...appeared on stage
I had one line in a school play and I still remember it. I was a space alien and I said, "Has earth got a dark half, like us?"

...wore make-up
When I was about two! I've always slapped it on and I first dyed my hair when I was twelve. My mum came home from work and I'd poured a bottle of peroxide all over my head. There was nothing she could do.

...stayed out all night
At a festival in Spain, when I was about eleven. I used to go on holiday with my family every year and there's a festival at San Lorenzo there every year for a week. There's loads of dancing in the streets and everyone stays out all night.

...fancied a pop star
George Michael. I was going to marry him, but I think that's a challenge I won't be able to fulfil!

...went to a football match
I went to see Watford not that long ago. It was quite good fun. I was watching it for the wrong reasons, though – looking at the players and deciding whether I fancied them or not. Still, it's quite an interesting game and I got into it – I do see there's skill involved, as well.

...saw a live concert
Wham! George Michael pointed in my direction and sang, "And all I want right now is you". I thought he meant it – I was only twelve!

...saw a 15 film
I was twelve and stuffed my bra up with socks and put on loads of make-up. I was short for my age, so I thought all the other girls would get in and I wouldn't. But I did – and saw 'Desperately Seeking Susan'.

...went abroad
To Spain at an early age.

...had a near-death experience
The first time I ever went freestyle skiing cross country and I thought, yeah, I can do this! I got stuck at the top of a mountain and nearly fell over a crevice. It was really, really scary, but I managed to save myself!

...wore a mini skirt
When I was about nine. I remember playing a game called 'True Dare, Double Dare, Love, Kiss or Promise' and I got to snog this boy in the stock room cupboard. I was sure that it was my mini skirt that did it!

...killed an animal
My brother and I were in a gang and we used to lift up the tiles in the back garden and pour petrol on the woodlice underneath, set light to them and burn them.

...got drunk
When I was thirteen, I won a bottle of Pomagne at the school fete and I drank the whole thing myself.

...won a prize
When I swam my 20 metres I got a certificate, but other than that it was with Spice Girls.

...went to hospital
During a video shoot, I was picking my ear and my finger had a false nail on it. The nail fell down my ear and got stuck and I had to get it removed in hospital.

...fell in love
It was infatuated love – when I was about sixteen – with this guy who it turned out had snogged my mate as well.

"I think the way we are rubs off on other people. Because It's healthy. If you spend a while with us, you'll soon be running

"My greatest extravagance is talking openly and honestly

everyone wants to run down a corridor naked. around with all your bits bobbing about."

to someone who won't kiss and tell."

was Girl Power. But the point is that Girl Power isn't about dictating how people should be. It's about taking control of your own destiny. Some people don't get it and it's when people misunderstand the message that I get upset.

"The papers are probably to blame for that. When I said Margaret Thatcher was the first Spice Girl I wasn't claiming I was a real Tory. I just admire people with ideals. Even if it's not my point of view I respect the fact that it takes dedication and guts to stand up and say what you believe in. I hate hypocrisy, so I have to stand up and say what I mean. And I'm ready to take the consequences.

"That's why I don't get upset when negative stories are written about me in the papers. Most of them are untrue anyway, but I knew that things like that could happen when I chose to go into this career. One bloke said I slept with him when all I ever did was kiss him on the cheek! Can you believe that? The point is that today's news really is tomorrow's fish and chip paper, so the good of being a Spice Girl far outweighs the bad.

"I grew up in quite a poor family, but now I've got everything I could ever want as far as material goods are concerned. It's great to be able to buy nice things, but what I'm searching for is more spiritual. That's what we were put on the earth for originally; to improve our spirituality, not for material gain. I was just as happy as I am now when I was skint. I've lived on less than 30 quid a week and had just as much of a laugh.

"I've got two tattoos now because I think they're very spiritual too. I had them done to prove to myself that I could endure the pain. It's a ritual thing and they help tell the story of my life. I recently had a sundial design at the top of my

"I come from a neurotic turbulent family. If you wanted to get deep and psychological about it, you could say that for many reasons I wanted to be heard."

"I'm sure people see me as a screaming redhead with a big pair of boobs, but I like to think I've got things to say."

"Spice Girls are about freedom of expression, which is why we wanted to retain our own personalities. We don't need a uniform to show we have something in common."

back, while the first one I had was a Jaguar further down in memory of my dad, who was a car dealer and drove a Jaguar. He died three years ago and it's my greatest regret that he isn't here today to see what's happened to me in Spice Girls.

"I think a lot of the troubles that we have today stem from young people not being allowed to dream. If a kid at school says he wants to be a spaceman when he grows up, then he shouldn't be told not to be so stupid. The Careers Officer should say, 'OK, then. First you'll have to learn about astrophysics' or whatever. We need more people to say that anything is possible.

"I'm the proof that dreams can come true. I love people coming up to me in the street because that's the purest gratification I can get. I'd hate myself if I didn't have time for those people, because they've given me everything.

"What have I bought so far? Well, I now drive an MGB 1967 Roadster convertible with silver spokes, like you see in all the classic Bond movies. The engine sounds like my voice when I've been out all night, really throaty. Or like Rod Stewart singing 'Baby Jane'! I liked him when he used to wear those leopard-skin pants. I'm into trash. I guess I'm just a trashy kinda girl!"

"My idea of perfect happiness is complete inner peace. The traits I most deplore in others are preconceptions, prejudice and narrow-mindedness."

THE BIG QUESTIONS?

Whose toothbrush would you least like to borrow?
Mel C: The bloke on 'Coronation Street' who makes the pies and asked Rita to marry him.
Victoria: Rab C Nesbit.
Emma: Ken Dodd.
Geri: A tabloid photographer.
Mel B: Tommy Cooper.

Who would you most like to ram on the dodgems?
Mel C: Peter Schmeichel.
Victoria: Mark Morrison.
Emma: David Wicks from 'Eastenders' (I like him, but he's a bit naughty, so I'd like to give him a telling off, then a big kiss afterwards).
Geri: Not that I'm obsessed or anything, but a tabloid photographer.
Mel B: No one I can particularly think of.

Who would you most like to get stuck in a fridge with?
Mel C: Ron from 'Eastenders' (to keep me warm).
Victoria: Stephen Dorff (I'd

Which TV doctor would you most like to operate on you?
Mel C: George Clooney from 'ER'.
Victoria: George Clooney (and I hope it would be an internal!)
Emma: George Clooney
Geri: Dr. Who – all five of them!
Mel B: Dr. Legg from 'Eastenders'.

Who would you least like to see you on the loo?
Mel C: My dad.
Victoria: Stephen Dorff.
Emma: A nun who taught me at school.
Geri: A tabloid photographer.
Mel B: I don't mind who sees me on the toilet.

Who would you least like to suck your toes?
Mel C: Anyone I fancy.
Victoria: Trevor MacDonald.
Emma: Ken Dodd.
Geri: I wouldn't mind anyone sucking my toes because if I didn't like them, I just wouldn't wash my feet that day!
Mel B: My grandad.

74

want someone I could be passionate with, because if you're stuck in a fridge there's a good chance you're not getting out alive).
Emma: Dawn French.
Geri: Antonio Banderas.
Mel B: Will Smith from 'Fresh Prince of Bel Air'. He's very nice.

Which chef would you most like to cook for you?

Mel C: Ainsley. Even though he's really annoying, I like him.
Victoria: Lenny Henry.

Emma: My dad.
Geri: Keith Floyd, and we'd get drunk together.
Mel B: Mr Chippy in Leeds. He does wicked chips cooked perfectly and really nice batter on the fish, and specially nice scraps.

Which superhero would you most like to spend the day with?

Mel C: Spiderman, so I could get caught up in his web!
Victoria: Batman, but it would have to be Val Kilmer.
Emma: Superman, so we

could fly together.
Geri: Wonderwoman.
Mel B: Nelson Mandela (does he count?).

Which is your favourite football team

Mel C: Liverpool, of course.
Victoria: Manchester United.
Emma: Tottenham and Liverpool.
Geri: I've got a soft spot for Kevin Phillips. He plays for Watford and he's really cute.
Mel B: Leeds United.

That's it...

...for our very first book – hope you enjoyed being Spiced! Putting it all together was a wicked experience for us – a brilliant opportunity to tell it like it is (and kick all the rip-offs out of the shops into the bargain!)

Remember, if it doesn't say OFFICIAL on the front, then it's nothing to do with us – and that goes for all those crappy excuses for magazines you see on the shelves, too. Don't buy them! They're overpriced and don't say anything new – a waste of your hard-earned dosh! If you want more Spice, then join our Spice Girls Magazine Club (see the last page for details). Written and edited by us, the Spice Girls, just for you, it's got all the inside information you're dying to know, plus personal pictures you won't see anywhere else!

This year is shaping up to be our most exciting yet. Recently we signed an amazing deal with Pepsi, which is great for us and good news for our fans because it means we'll be able to give away loads of fab freebies over the coming months. Then, in the summer we're planning to go back into the studio to record our new album. At the moment, we're throwing around loads of ideas – with all the travelling we've done over the last twelve months, we want to take our influences from all over the world. We're thinking of doing a Bhangra tune and we also want to do a number with a big brass band behind us. Plus, we've just heard that this summer we're off to shoot a Spice Girls movie... so watch this space.

But what we're most psyched up about it next year's mega World Tour, which starts in February – it's going to be totally wicked and exciting! As far as we're concerned, that's what all this hard work has been for. It's the same for all of us – getting up on stage is the best feeling in the world and we just can't wait! Hope you'll join us! In the meantime, you know what to do... Spice it up, big time!

Thanks for buying the book,

Lots of love...

**EMMA
MEL B
GERI
MEL C
VICTORIA**

COMING SOON!

ONE HOUR OF GIRL POWER!
THE OFFICIAL VIDEO - VOLUME 1

SPICE GIRLS OFFICIAL COLLECTION

MINI RUCKSACK

COFFEE MUG

A4 RING FILE

SILVER RING

PLASTIC KEYRING

"SPICEWATCH" POSTER

Name.. PLEASE USE BLOCK CAPITALS

Address..

....Postcode...

IF PAYING BY VISA/ACCESS CARD NUMBER IS:

☐☐☐☐ ☐☐☐☐ ☐☐☐☐ ☐☐☐☐ Signature...Card expiry Date....................

How To Order

Ordering is easy. You can place your order by post or telephone, and can pay by cheque, postal order or credit card. Please print your order clearly and remember to add the correct postage and packing charge. Items ordered together are not necessarily shipped together. All out of stock items will be shipped immediately upon arrival of stock. Your credit card will only be charged after an item is shipped

By telephone 0990 24 21 18

You may telephone your order quoting your credit card details for payment 9AM-8PM. Seven days per week.

By Post

Fill in this order form

Include payment. Sorry no cash

Send to: Spice Girls Merchandising, P.O. BOX 13, Borehamwood, Herts, WD6 3BS.

Make cheques and postal orders payable to: Spice Girls Merchandising.

Please allow 28 days for delivery. Orders from outside the UK are subject to an extra charge of £1 per item to cover the extra costs of administration and shipments. Payment for overseas orders should be in Sterling. Overseas orders may attract local taxes which will be the responsibility of the customer. Delivery time could exceed 28 days outside the UK.

ITEM	CODE	PRICE (£)	QTY	TOTAL
1. MINI RUCKSACK	1001	19.99		
2. COFFEE MUG	1009	5.99		
3. A4 RING FILE	1004	4.99		
4. SILVER RING	1006	9.99		
5. PLASTIC KEYRING	1002	1.99		
6. POSTER (36"X24")	1008	4.99		

PLEASE ADD POSTAGE & PACKAGING: UP TO £15, £1.50 (EUROPE £2.50)
PLEASE ADD POSTAGE & PACKAGING: UP TO £30, £1.90 (EUROPE £2.90)
PLEASE ADD POSTAGE & PACKAGING: UP TO £50, £2.50 (EUROPE £3.50)
PLEASE ADD POSTAGE & PACKAGING: OVER £50, £4.00 (EUROPE £5.00)

POST & PACKAGING: £ ☐   **TOTAL:** £ ☐

IF YOU DON'T WANT TO TEAR THIS PAGE TO SEND IN, EITHER ORDER BY TELEPHONE

0990 24 21 18

OR PHOTOCOPY IT AND SEND TO

SPICE GIRLS MERCHANDISING, P.O. BOX 13, BOREHAMWOOD, HERTS, WD6 3BS

LOOK OUT FOR A BRAND NEW RANGE OF SPICE GIRLS T-SHIRTS IN APRIL PHONE 0990 24 21 18 FOR DETAILS

GIRL POWER IS COMING AT YOU!

Don't miss out!
Get with the vibe... join the spiciest new gang around...

THE ONLY OFFICIAL GIRL POWER MAGAZINE

SPICE

Issue 1
£2.50

WRITTEN BY THE SPICE GIRLS JUST FOR YOU!

"Take control!"
How girl power can change your life

COVER PHOTOGRAPH by Ellen Von Unwerth

THE 1997  SPICE GIRLS
MAGAZINE CLUB

HERE'S WHAT HAPPENS WHEN YOU JOIN:

GET SPICE: SPICE is the only magazine written by the Spice Girls, just for you! For £10, we'll send you four issues over the next year. No other magazine has the real inside information on the band and exclusive photos. Accept no substitute! You can't be spiced without it!

READ IT HERE FIRST... SPICE gives you the latest on where the Spice Girls are at, including details on events, new releases and remixes. You don't want to miss out on the spiciest parts of life, so make sure you hear all the news first in **SPICE**!

HOW TO JOIN: Send your cheque/postal order for £10, along with your name and address to:
SPICE GIRLS MAGAZINE CLUB, PO BOX 11932, LONDON SW11 4ZN

THE ONE & ONLY • THE ONE & ONLY • THE ONE & ONLY • THE ONE &
official SPICE magazine